Deaf History Notes

by
Brian Cerney, Ph.D.

Table of Contents

Contents 3

This book was created out of a need to guide my students who were studying ASL and the interpreting process. I wanted them to move toward a greater understanding of the history of the American Deaf Community, American Sign Language, and how language, culture, and social pressures all affect the work of bilingual, bicultural mediation – Interpreting. The result has been this book, which in its first version was only about twenty pages long, but kept growing semester after semester as I included more and more information.

I have segmented this work into six Units. It is intended that students would work their way, in order, from the first Unit to the Sixth Unit. I have also divided each Unit into separate, easily readable (I hope), segments. This allows an instructor to target certain areas and even ignore others very easily. It also provides a targeted approach so that all of the related information for a segment is easily found together. I have included questions at the beginning and end of each Unit to help students further understand, analyze and synthesize the content of each Unit. Students are exposed to semiotics (the study of communication) linguistics (the study of language), sociology (the study of human social structure) and anthropology (the study of humans and their cultural development) without being overwhelmed by big labels like "Semiotics" or "Linguistics"[1]

At the beginning of each Unit are these big-picture concepts. Unit One, for example, starts out by describing the properties of communication and language, then identifies the events which fostered the creation of American Sign Language. Unit Two begins by talking about language policies and oppression, then identifies the events and organizations which played a role in the battle over the use of signed languages in educational institutions. Unit Three begins by exploring the pathological view of deafness and examining the ethics of science and research to promote specific viewpoints; then explores the anatomy related to signed languages. Unit Four introduces the reader to the power of linguistics as a tool for fostering cultural identity and also explores language variety within the Deaf community. Unit Five compares the concepts of empowerment and paternalism. Unit Six introduces the reader to the profession of interpreting and the keys to being a professional interpreter of ASL and English in the United States.

Throughout this text I intend to keep the information clear and easily understandable. There is no need to use thirty words to explain something when fifteen will do. I do consider this text permanently under revision. So please take the time to tell me if a sentence was hard to read or if any facts are either confusing or just plain wrong. It is through communication that we learn and improve; I do not intend the communication contained in this book to be only one-way. Check the publisher's web site for instructions on how to send your comments to me.

I hope you actually enjoy this text and I also hope that you enjoy any course work connected with it. Your exploration of the Deaf community only begins and ends where you set your own limits. Make the decision to remove all boundaries from your potential; and let the adventure begin!

---

[1] The fact that you are actually READING this preface proves that you are such a diligent student that you would never be overwhelmed with big labels ... but DON'T tell your classmates that this book exposes them to such "ivory tower" concepts as Sociology and Anthropology! (shhhh!)

The Origins of American Sign Language

Chilmark [is] an "up-island" town in the southwest part
of Martha's Vineyard. It's a town of rolling hills,
threaded with stone walls; of undulating sandy cliffs
offering sweeping views of the Atlantic Ocean.   Over
those hills the wind blows soft and sometimes howls.
The ocean rushes onto the shore at Windy Gates and
bubbles over the rock-strewn beach at Squibnocket.   On
murky days foghorns warn boats off.   Always there are
the sounds of seagulls, bell buoys, the wind, the surf.

 If you lived in Chilmark in the 18th or 19th century,
up to a quarter of your neighbors never heard these
sounds.   And in a place that was itself isolated — a
trip "down-island" took a day over rutted roads — the
deaf of Chilmark could have been excruciatingly lonely.
Yet they lived full lives, grew up, were happy or
unhappy, farmed well or farmed poorly, married well or
badly, and got on or didn't get on with their neighbors
like anybody else.   They just spoke with their hands.
(Jamie Kageleiry, 1999:52)

Martha's Vineyard represents part of the origins of American Sign Language. A school in Paris, France also plays a large role and so does a young man in his mid twenties who stumbles upon a deaf girl in Connecticut. The intertwining of these pieces represents the beginnings of the most widely known signed language on Earth.

This Unit explores the differences between communication and language and the reasons that American Sign Language is a legitimate language. You will discover the importance of Residential Schools to the stabilization of new signed languages and to the wide-spread use of signed languages within large geographical regions. You will also discover the origins of American Sign Language.

Look for the answers to the following questions as you read:

1)   What are the similarities and differences between communication and language?

2)   How are expressive and perceptive modalities of communication linked?

3)   What requirements must be present before a communication system can be considered a language?

4)   What are language Modalities, language Channels, and Language Encoding Systems?

5)   Identify several language modalities for each of the three language channels.

6)   Who conducted the initial research of ASL that met these requirements?

7)   How did Spanish Catholic monks impact Deaf education?

8)   How did the first public school for deaf children in the world come into existence?

9)   What role did this school have upon the stabilization of French Sign Language?

10)   Who was the first deaf person to teach deaf students?

11)   Who was the first deaf person to teach American deaf students?

12)   What educational experiences did these two teachers have in common?

13)   What role did French Sign Language play in the formation of American Sign Language?

14)   What role did the signed language of Martha's Vineyard play in the formation of ASL?

15)   How did the first permanent school for deaf children in the United States come into existence?

16)   What role did this school have upon the stabilization of American Sign Language?

Section 1 – Communication & Language
Communication

\What does it mean to communicate? **Communication is one mind's perception of a message that another mind has expressed.** Communication can be immediate – such as seeing someone smile or saying hello; or delayed – such as seeing an arrow painted on a tree or an old sign which describes an historical landmark. Communication takes place between living things, but it is not limited to humans. Most (if not all) animals have the ability to communicate. Animals can indicate that they are angry or injured. They can stake out territory, seek and find mates, issue warnings, and indicate submission. Some forms of communication are more complex than others: Many mammals are able to growl and bare their teeth to communicate a threat or warning to a potential foe. Bees can indicate sources of pollen through complex dances. Whales are said to produce a new complex song every year that is shared throughout their species. Human beings who share no language in common with each other are still able to bargain and negotiate over the cost of a piece of pottery. Communication simply requires at least two minds and some way of expressing and perceiving information between those two minds.

Communication is a broad category that includes all possibilities of language; but communication includes much, much more than only language. Animals have the ability to communicate at least within their species and generally between species. Humans, being a specific kind of animal, share some of these communication abilities; but humans are able to move *beyond* mere communication when they use *language*. Figure 1.1 shows the relationships between animal communication, human communication, and language.

Figure 1.1 - Communication and Language

Communication begins with the intentions to communicate. This requires intelligence and therefore a brain, or mind, capable of thought and knowledge. The mind's intention, or meaning, may be either *Conscious* or *Unconscious*. Conscious intentions, where the mind is aware of its own intentions to communicate, are the most easily recognized. Requesting assistance, issuing a warning, or expressing affection are all possible conscious intentions for communication, especially when words are used such as "give me a hand, please", "back off!", or "you're so sweet!"

Unconscious intentions, where the mind is not directly aware of its own intentions to communicate, are less obvious. A request for assistance may be expressed as simply as a glance toward a nearby person. A warning can consist of a fierce stare. An expression of affection may be communicated by the dilation of pupils (of the eyes) when a certain person comes into view. Vocal inflections or facial expressions can also reveal unconscious intentions. People who are lying often find it difficult to make direct eye contact with the people they are lying to. A liar is usually not aware of the fact that his body is warning us not to believe what he is saying. In many cultures a nodding head is an indicator of truthfulness. Shaking one's head side to side while strongly affirming a statement (such as is commonly seen in advertising, e.g. "I use it every day!") may be a result of the person's subconscious expression of communication. Their words say "I use this product every day" but their body language says "I am not telling you the truth." A child may state that she is "not scared" but her vocal inflection and facial expression reveal that she is actually quite frightened. Our *unconscious mind* is almost always expressing our *emotional state*. Our *conscious mind* provides the ability to communicate things *beyond emotion*.

The Four Components of Communication

Four components are always present in any act of communication: 1) Background Knowledge of Participants, 2) Expressive Modalities of Communication, 3) Perceptive Modalities of Communication, and 4) Physical Context.. An understanding of each of these variables will make us more aware of the communication that can co-occur with language and help us understand the truthfulness or emotion surrounding a message.

Background Knowledge is all the information that a person (or animal) has. Background Knowledge can help us to understand the topic of discussion, to make predictions about how it might be organized, and to know when communication is inappropriate for the situation at hand. If we fail to consider another person's background knowledge then we might confuse them by giving them too much new information in a lecture or bore them by repeating things that they already know. Figure 1.2 shows the mind (human or animal) and some of the various kinds of background information that can influence communication.

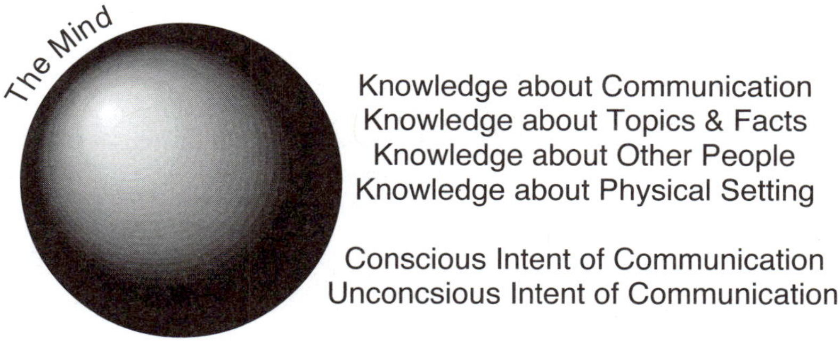

The Mind

Knowledge about Communication
Knowledge about Topics & Facts
Knowledge about Other People
Knowledge about Physical Setting

Conscious Intent of Communication
Unconcsious Intent of Communication

Figure 1.2 - Background Knowledge

Expressive Modalities of Communication are all the ways that a person creates communication, whether by making a sound, drawing a picture, nodding one's head, or making eye contact. *All conscious expressive modalities of communication require muscle movement.* It is possible to use several expressive modalities of communication at the same time: a person may gesture to indicate that an unseen person is able to overhear the communication in a room (such as one's boss) while the conversation is conducted with the intention that the unseen person will "overhear" it. A deeper understanding of Expressive Modalities of Communication may help us detect conflicting information: a person's facial expression and body posture may indicate extreme anger while their words are produced with amazing calm. Conscious expressions of communication typically use speech, facial expressions, and manual gestures. Remember that these include things that are not words such as humming a song (such as the theme music from the "Jeopardy" game show to encourage someone to hurry up), rolling one's eyes in disbelief, or waving to greet a friend.

Unconscious expressions of communication are also possible. Linguists have discovered that people who are lying tend to avert eye gaze and raise their eyebrows during the lie. While these two expressions of communication require muscle movement another form may also happen when a person is lying: increased perspiration. For our purposes in contrasting communication and language we will focus only on the consciously controlled aspects of communication (those that require muscle movement). Figure 1.3 represents both the mind (with its background knowledge and communication intentions) and the various ways that the mind may express communication.

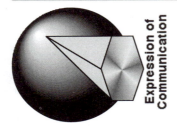

Expressive Modalities

- Auditory (speech, manual contact, etc)
- Visual (manual, non-manual)
- Tactile (manual, non-manual)
- Gustatory / Olfactory (taste & smell)

Figure 1.3 - Expressive Modalities of Communication

Perceptive Modalities of Communication are all the ways that a person receives information, whether by hearing, seeing, feeling, or even smelling or tasting. *All perceptive modalities of communication involve the senses.* Knowing about perceptive modalities helps us to analyze physical settings and eliminate potential sources of noise or disruption to the communication. It also helps us to understand potential mis-perceptions of information.

We may see a person smiling as we simultaneously hear them speak and feel their hand during a handshake. All of these perceptions would help us understand that we are being greeted; but we might also see and feel that their hands are cold and shaking and hear that their voice is not steady as they speak. These additional perceptions might indicate that the person is nervous or not feeling well. We may consciously perceive some parts of the communication while unconsciously perceiving others. It is often this unconscious perception which leads us to having a "gut instinct" not to trust someone or to think they might be lying to us. Figure 1.4 represents both the mind and the various ways that the mind may perceive communication.

**Perception of
Communication**

Perceptive Modalities

- Auditory (ears / hearing)
- Visual (eyes / sight)
- Tactile (skin / touch)
- Gustatory (tongue / taste)
- Olfactory (nose / smell)

Figure 1.4 - Perceptive Modalities of Communication

Physical Contexts are the places where communication takes place, whether in an auditorium, in a forest, free-falling 1,000 feet above the earth, or in a cave. Noisy physical contexts may make it difficult or impossible to communicate by sound. Dark physical contexts can prohibit visual communication. Physical contexts shape all of our communication not only because of potential noise, but also because certain settings are restricted to certain kinds of communication (and vice versa) such as sermons in a church, lectures in a classroom, or cheers at a basketball court.

Figure 1.5 represents two minds expressing and perceiving communication within a physical context.

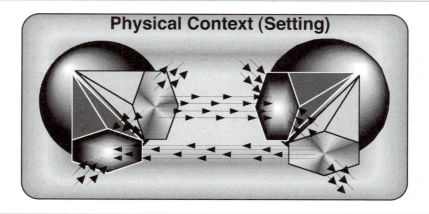

Figure 1.5 - Communication within a Physical Setting

Modes of Expressing and Perceiving Communication

Image, Sound, and Texture are the three most easily manipulated modalities for expressing communication. Images and Sight allow for visual communication. Non-linguistic visual communication includes eye contact, facial expressions, body postures, gestures, pictures or drawings, and written or printed symbols. The physical environment is largely perceived through sight as well. Communication about the physical environment to another person can be accomplished as simply as making eye contact with a person and looking at an immediate danger to that person (such as an oncoming car).

Visual information should be conveyed to blind people as part of interpretations. When English words such as "this" and "that" are used, they are often accompanied by gestures that identify the referent of each word. The body posture and facial expression of people can provide significant input to understanding a message. This information should be fully identified for a blind consumer to understand the message correctly. Knowing that a person has just raised her hand will help explain why a lecture comes to a sudden halt and the teacher asks "Do you have a question?"

Sound and Hearing allow for auditory communication. Non-linguistic auditory communication includes grunts, squeals, sighs, hiccups, humming, music, footsteps, rustling paper, banging doors, and kicking furniture. Sounds permeate almost every physical environment. Even very quiet rooms often have some hum or hiss such as from electrical lights or wind. A sigh may be an indication of frustration. Footsteps may indicate that someone is about to knock at the door. Rustling papers may indicate nervousness. Banging doors and kicking furniture may indicate anger. If an interpreter working with a deaf consumer does not provide access to these sounds, then the consumer is not receiving the same communication as hearing people who are in the room. These auditory environmental stimuli may seem trivial, but there have been many instances where a door being slammed shut was the impetus for an angry lecture about a person's attitude.

Think about the auditory information that is taken for granted. If someone knocks at a door, it is perfectly logical for someone inside the room to approach the door, ask who is there, and perhaps open the door. If you didn't hear the knock, it would seem bizarre that someone in the room arbitrarily decided to walk to the door, talk to it, and suddenly cause a person to appear at the moment that the door was opened. Knowing that there is a knock at the door clearly helps explain why a person is standing there when another person decides to open it.

Similarly, a person who is continuously coughing in the back of the room communicates several things with every cough: 1) the cougher is not feeling completely healthy, 2) the cougher might actually be very ill, 3) the cougher is still in the room and has not yet left. If the cougher decides to leave, you would understand that they may wish to get a drink of water and that they are not being deliberately rude. If at some point you are expected to meet and shake hands with each person in the room you may understand why the cougher does not shake hands with you (or you might consider washing your hands if the cougher does shake hands with you). If at some point another person asks the cougher to leave the room and get a drink of water, you will understand such a request to be fairly normal.

Touch and Texture allow for tactile communication. Non-linguistic tactile communication includes holding hands, giving a hug, pats on the back, tickling, massaging, punching, and scratching. Certain aspects of physical environments are perceived tactually including the temperature of the room. A warm room in the winter may indicate that one's host is concerned for her guests and wishes to ensure they are comfortable.

Our sense of smell and of taste can also contribute to perceptions of communication. The odor of perfume or the taste of your favorite meal can be meaningful. But we do not use odor or taste for communicating with language. Language is restricted to the three modalities of Image/Sight, Sound/Hearing, and Texture/Touch. The chart below gives some examples of Images, Sounds, and Textures that can communicate. Examples typed in UPPERCASE are specific examples of communication which are also examples of language.

Expressive / Perceptive Modalities of Communication		
Image / Sight	*Sound / Hearing*	*Texture / Touch*
• Drawings - cartoon figures - lifelike sketches • Markings - arrows - PRINTED WORDS	• Human Sounds - screams - SPOKEN WORDS • Mechanical Sounds - doors slamming shut -MORSE CODE TONES	• Objects - fences - sculptures • 3-D Markings - 3-D arrow on a sign - BRAILLED WORDS

Figure 1.6 - Examples of Communication Modalities

Language Versus Communication

Any animal may use 1)   *symbols* (such as sounds or body movements) to convey information between members of 2) *a community*, but the word *language* can only describe certain types of *human* communication systems. **Language** is a *specific kind of communication* that meets all four of these *additional* requirements:

3) The communication system must have rules for the sequencing of the symbols (ie. grammar).
4) The communication system must have an infinite number of ways to encode any given message.
5) The communication system must pass between at least two generations of active users.
6) The communication system must be flexible enough to accept change over time and between users.

In sum, **language is the *systematic* use of *symbols* to express and perceive information between members of a *community* in which the system is *rule-governed*, has *infinite production* possibilities, is *intergenerational*, and *changes over time*.** Humans are the only species on Earth that have demonstrated the ability to communicate via language.

The Three Language Channels

Now that we understand language as a subset of communication, we can further explore a few more ideas about language. To begin, let's consider the three possible language channels. **Language Channels are the three basic ways of expressing language: signed, spoken, and written.** English has two language channels (written English and spoken English) while American Sign Language currently has only one channel (signed ASL) but may some day adopt one of several writing systems proposed for ASL (although none are widely used at this time). Channels and Modes are related, but not as a one-to-one match. Generally, a spoken language is encoded through the modality of sound; written and signed languages are usually encoded through the modality of images. But spoken languages can be encoded visually via shorthand or manual cues. Written symbols can be spelled aloud or transformed into Morse code tones. Texture is a common language-encoding mechanism for blind and DeafBlind people and can easily encode signed, spoken, or written language channels. The point where language channel and modality converge is called Language Encoding Systems.

Multiple Language Encoding Systems

As we have seen above, the three channels of written language, signed language, and spoken language can be expressed through image, sound, or texture. Within the channel of writing we might first think of printing or cursive writing; but it is also possible to express written languages through dots and dashes for Morse Code or through raised dots on a flat surface for Braille. Morse Code and Braille are not languages – they are Language Encoding Systems. **Language Encoding Systems** are finite and closed sets of symbols which express the basic structural components of a language. If those symbols (letters of the alphabet, dots and dashes) are embossed so that they can be detected by touch alone, they still encode a written channel but the expressive modality is texture and the perceptive modality is touch. Speech is a Language Encoding System that can encode any spoken languages; Braille, Morse code, semaphore, printing and cursive writing are Language Encoding Systems which can encode any written language; and Signing is a Language Encoding System which can encode any signed language. If you know a language, then you know at least one Language Encoding System for it. If you did not know any Language Encoding Systems then you could not encode or perceive any languages at all. The chart below identifies a few examples of the different modalities that can encode each language channel.

Language Channels	Expressive / Perceptive Modalities		
	Image / Sight	*Sound / Hearing*	*Texture / Touch*
Written Languages	• Typed Symbols • Morse Code Symbols	• Morse Code Tones • Spelling Aloud	• Brailled Symbols • Raised Letters
Signed Languages	• Signed Symbols		• Tactile Signing
Spoken Languages	• Phonetic Alphabets • Manual Cues	• Spoken Symbols	• Tadoma • Tactile Manual Cues

Figure 1.7 - Language Encoding Systems

Identifying Communication as Language – The Case for ASL

Prior to 1960, the definition of language specifically excluded gestural communication systems. There was a widely held belief that languages could not include gestural communication and therefore was limited to written or spoken communication. In the late 1950's, William Stokoe [STO-kee] became the first person to systematically study a signed language. William Stokoe was an English professor at Gallaudet College. He was certain that there was structure to the signing his Deaf students used and that this structure was independent of English.

Stokoe began his investigation by exploring the first part of the definition of language. Specifically, **Stokoe analyzed the rules for the formation and organization of the symbols used in American Sign Language**. In 1960 he published a research article entitled *Sign Language Structure*. In that article, Stokoe identified three basic elements which come together to form signs: **location, handshape, and movement.** By 1974 other researchers – James Woodward (1973) and Robbin Battison (1974) – had identified a fourth element: **palm orientation.** These four elements of sign structure are known as the primary *FOUR PARAMETERS* of signed languages. They are essential elements of producing any sign in any signed language. Stokoe later expressed the parameters of signed languages as an even simpler notion of two things: *actor* and *action*. In other words, something acts (a hand at the side of the head, the muscles in the cheek to one side of the nose) and an action takes place (the tip of the hand taps the side of the forehead, the cheek muscle contracts and "wrinkles" one side of the nose).

Stokoe also was the first to identify the signed language in the United States as "American Sign Language" (ASL). His work paved the way for other researchers to complete the picture and prove beyond all doubt that American Sign Language is a legitimate language, as rich and complex as Spanish, Russian, Chinese, or Swahili. Following Stokoe's lead, other researchers identified the rules for ordering the signs (grammar), the ability to follow the rules while encoding the same message in an infinite number of ways (productivity), the fact that the language has been handed down through multiple generations of users (intergenerational transmission), and the ability for the language to adapt and change over time (chronological change).

1) **ASL has a system of creating symbols**
2) **ASL is shared by a community of users**
3) **ASL has rules governing the sequences of symbols**
4) **ASL has infinite production possibilities**
5) **ASL has been passed down across generations**
6) **ASL has changed with use across time**

Thus, ASL meets all the requirements necessary to identify a language. These requirements were established by linguists and have been applied to spoken languages long before anyone analyzed a signed language to determine whether signed languages would follow these rules. As a result of Stokoe's research, people began to understand that speech is not the only way for language to be produced; they began to accept the possibility that signing was a possible language channel.

With ASL meeting all six of the requirements to be considered a language, the old expectation that language must also be spoken has since been eliminated. Linguists around the world now acknowledge rule-governed signed communication systems as languages. Although William Stokoe was the person who gave the name "American Sign Language" to the signed language of the United States of America and most of Canada, other signed languages have different symbols, and different rules, than ASL. These other signed languages generally reflect the names of the countries or provinces in which the language is used such as British Sign Language, Australian Sign Language, French Sign Language, Italian Sign Language, Quebec Sign Language, etc. So far there have been no signed languages that have been shown to follow exactly the same rules for any spoken language. In other words, French Sign Language (LSF) is not based upon spoken French; and Italian Sign Language (LSI) is not based upon spoken Italian. These names of these signed languages simply indicate that the people who use LSF generally reside in France and the people who use LSI generally reside in Italy. Likewise the title ASL identifies that the users of the language generally reside in North America.

ASL Is Not A *Universal* Language

ASL is still the most widely recognized and researched signed language so far, but there are probably as many signed languages as there are spoken languages. ASL has historical connections to French Sign Language and many similarities between the two languages remain. There are many similarities among most European signed languages and these relationships are due to the School for the Deaf in Paris, France. No two of these signed languages are mutually intelligible, but the similarities in certain vocabulary items parallel the similarities between Spanish, French, Italian, and Portuguese (all of which have historical links to Latin and the Roman Empire). Signed languages in the European family share common links to French Sign Language and the Paris School for the Deaf. Educators from all over Europe traveled to the school, stayed, learned some amount of French Sign Language, and returned to their native countries to start educating deaf children. The French Sign Language of the teachers merged with the indigenous signs of the deaf people in each country. Thus each European signed language is unique, yet each has its own similarities with French Sign Language.

American Sign Language has changed significantly over time. Prior to the 1800's deaf people in the United States may have had a variety of local signed languages, each different from the other. In 1817 the sign language of Martha's Vineyard merged with

French Sign Language to establish a new and independent language, which we now know as American Sign Language. The next chapter explores the origins of the Paris school and its impact upon the signed languages across Europe and the United States. The rest of this unit explains how these two languages came into contact and the greatest force leading to the solidification of all national signed languages - residential schools for Deaf children.

Section 2 – Deaf Education & Language Stability
Pedro Ponce DeLeón and Private Education for Deaf Children

The earliest recorded mentioning of deaf people and their use of signed languages comes from Greek society and the age of philosophers. Plato's "Cratylus" dialogue quotes Socrates as having stated "If we had neither voice nor tongue, and yet wished to manifest things to one another, should we not, like those which are at present mute, endeavor to signify our meaning by the hands, head, and other parts of the body?" Aristotle would later note that "Those who are born deaf all become speechless, they have a voice, but are destitute of speech." Later Galen, the Greek physician, hypothesized that speech and hearing had the same source in the brain and that damage to one function ensured damage to the other. No significant challenges to these beliefs would take place for centuries. The change finally began in the 1500s.

The motivation for teaching deaf children has its roots in two areas: religion and money. Religion is involved in that Christianity works toward spreading the news of the Gospel to all the earth. Hebrew tradition prohibited most people with disabilities from entering the temple, yet deaf people were allowed to enter. But in the Catholic church of sixteenth-century Spain a person had to be able to make confession by speech. It was this very requirement that had prohibited Gaspard Burgos, a deaf man, from becoming a Benedictine monk. Pedro Ponce DeLeón, a Benedictine monk, apparently took interest in Burgos and is reported to have taught Burgos to speak and to write.

Money enters the picture due to the fact that sixteenth-century Spain was a world-dominating power that was colonizing much of Central and South America. One result of these efforts was the incredible fortunes of gold being returned to the wealthy elite of Spanish society. With the Spanish nobility striving to maintain its fortunes, intermarriage of extended family members was common. If each parent carried recessive genes for deafness then intermarriage increased the likelihood that some of their children would be born deaf. Indeed, this did happen and there was a great concern that arose because Spanish law (based in ancient Roman law) required a person to be able to speak in order to inherit the family's fortunes or to create a will to pass it on to the next generation. The deaf children of Spanish nobility needed to learn how to speak in order to preserve the families' riches.

So Pedro Ponce DeLeón was put to the task of privately teaching some of Spain's elite deaf children. By means of fingerspelling and writing he worked toward the goal of the children learning to read, write, and speak. Apparently he did not pursue the issue of lipreading with much interest, nor is there any record of him using a signed language to provide his instruction. Records indicate that around 1570 he was teaching a total of four deaf children of the Spanish elite.

Upon DeLeon's death in 1584, Juan Pablo Bonet and Emanuel Ramirez de Carrión continued to use DeLeón's methods for the private instruction of deaf children. Bonet became involved by working for the Constable of Castile, who was the great-nephew of three of DeLeón's students. The Constable's brother was deaf. While there is no clear record that Bonet ever directly educated any deaf children, he did manage to publish a text in 1620 that described the methods of instruction, including the one-handed manual alphabet. The alphabet pictured in his text bears significant resemblance to one published more than forty years previously. Legend suggests that this one-handed alphabet (which is the basis for ASL's fingerspelling) was originally created and used by Spanish monks who otherwise maintained a vow of silence.

Abbé de l'Epée and Public Education for Deaf Children

The Abbé de l'Epée lived in Paris, France during the 1700's. In 1760 he encountered twin sisters who were deaf. The girls were fifteen but had no form of education other than that of a priest who had attempted to teach them about the saints through pictures. The priest had died and the girls' mother asked de l'Epée to help teach her daughters. He taught them in his home by first having them teach him their signed language. He did not recognize that signed languages had the richness and complexity of spoken languages. He believed that signed languages could not convey abstract thoughts. De l'Epée decided to supplement French Sign Language with signs he invented in order to convey grammatical parts of spoken French. He then placed the signs in French word order and thus created his "methodical signs."

L'Epée would provide public demonstrations of his methods and in 1776 he published a description of his methods. This openness was unique because most education for deaf children at that time was conducted as private business with secret methodologies. Those educators with secret methods and profit in mind looked upon deaf children as automatons who simply needed to be trained in lipreading and speech production. L'Epée recognized that deaf people could be truly educated, not merely trained. He holds a place of honor in the hearts of deaf people because he began the first free school for the education of deaf people, which was called the National Institution for Deaf-Mutes.

L'Epée's school was very successful. Deaf people from all over France would attend the school. Educators from across France studied at the National Institution and then established more schools throughout France. In this way the National Institution was a key element in the stabilization of French Sign Language (LSF). Now there was truly such a thing as French Sign Language rather than the signing of Paris, the signing of Lyon, the signing of Calais, etc. The key to successfully creating a single national language was first bringing deaf children together, exposing them to a cohesive model of accessible language, and then letting them (the deaf children) develop and expand the language naturally.

Eventually similar schools were also established throughout Europe, all based on l'Epée's teachings. Educators who wished to learn more about how to teach deaf people came to observe l'Epée's methods and his students' success, then returned to their home countries to begin new schools. In this way a certain amount of the signed language used in France was carried to each of the new schools set up throughout Europe. The result is a similarity of certain signs in Europe and also North America. But these similarities are not anything close to a universal signed language. Each signed language remains mutually unintelligible between the different language users. Only a limited amount of vocabulary is shared between any two. One study done of 256 vocabulary items for basic concepts (colors, numbers, emotions, family relations, basic actions) identified only two signs that had "universal" similarities across just seven different signed languages (Cerney, 1987). The two concepts that were produced similarly were "stand" and the number "five".

The unique differences that emerged in each signed language are due to the fact that in each place that a new school was established, the deaf people already had their own various signed languages. With the introduction of a central school into each country, a number of different signing varieties combined with the educational signing brought from France and created, more or less, a new standard signed language for each school region. There are many signed languages in Europe and North America. In several countries, such as Belgium and Canada, there are at least two distinct signed languages in wide use among different groups of deaf people. Belgium has Flemish Sign Language and Waloon Sign Language. Canada has American Sign Language and Quebec Sign Language.

The Abbé Sicard and Jean Massieu

When the Abbé de l'Epée started teaching other people how to teach deaf children, one of these new teachers was the Abbé Sicard. Sicard had trained in Paris and then established a school at Bordeaux, France. One of Sicard's methods of teaching was to bridge the understanding of signed language to the understanding of written language. Sicard would draw outlines of various objects and would then write the name of the object within the outline drawing. Each word would be introduced by using the actual object, the sign for the object, and the picture with the written word of the object. In this way Sicard was able to directly and visually expose his pupils to written French. One deaf student who was educated under Sicard was named Jean Massieu. Massieu was one of six deaf children and they used their own form of signing within the family. When Massieu was nearly fourteen he went to Sicard's school in Bordeaux. There he learned how to read, write, and count.

When the Abbé de l'Epée was dying, the Monseigneur Champion de Cicé sent Sicard with the news that l'Epée's school would continue under the Assembly's protection. After l'Epée died, in 1789[2], Sicard took over the Paris school. Under Sicard's direction, the school prospered and more educators flocked to Paris to learn l'Epée's and Sicard's methods. Now there were over fifty schools throughout Europe based on the Paris school's teachings. Jean Massieu moved with Sicard to Paris. Soon, Massieu began teaching other deaf children at the school and became the first educator of deaf people who was deaf himself.

There was great political turmoil during Sicard's time as director of the Paris school. The French Revolution had begun the same year that l'Epée died (1789) and would continue for ten years until 1799 when Napoleon Bonaparte returned from military campaigns in Egypt to seize control of the French government. In 1791 the government made the Paris school the official National Institute for deaf education and Sicard remained in charge.

The "First French Republic" was formed in 1792. Marie Antoinette and King Louis XIV were both executed on January 21st, 1793[3]. Soon afterward was the reign of terror where many noblemen were also executed. There was a general distrust of the church and its representatives. Sicard was imprisoned many times as a member of the clergy but each time Massieu came to his rescue. Massieu's intelligence and patience impressed the revolutionary leaders. Massieu had gained much respect for both himself and his teacher, Sicard. It was largely due to Sicard's writings and Massieu's teaching ability that the Paris school continued to grow and continued to influence new schools that were being established throughout Europe.

---

[2] 1789 is also the year that George Washington was inaugurated at the first President of the United States.
[3] By January of 1793, Washington had won re-election as President.

Following Massieu's footsteps were many other deaf children who would become teachers of even more deaf children. In less than half a century the abilities of deaf people had changed considerably. Once thought of as uneducable, Epée and Sicard had demonstrated that deaf children could not only be taught how to write Latin, French, and any other written language, but they could also learn how to perform mathematical calculations, how to debate philosophical issues and were even in the position of teaching other deaf children how to do the same. One of Massieu's deaf students who would himself become a teacher of even more deaf children was Laurent Clerc.

Laurent Clerc and Thomas Hopkins Gallaudet

Laurent Clerc was born in La Balme, France on December 26, 1785. When he was one year old he was left alone momentarily in a chair by the fireplace. He fell and burned his face. His parents discovered later that he was deaf and blamed the deafness on the fall, although it is highly uncommon to become deaf merely from falling. Most likely Laurent had been born deaf or had become deaf due to some early childhood illness but his deafness was not noticed until Laurent was older and was noticeably not developing speech or responding to environmental sounds.

Attempts at cures were tried with no success. Laurent's siblings used home signs to communicate. His parents did not. Clerc's father was the mayor, thus concerned with respect and dignity. When he learned of a school for deaf children in Paris he decided to send Laurent there, but instead of traveling himself, he had Laurent's uncle accompany the nearly twelve-year old Laurent on the week-long trip. He would spend most of the next twenty years of his life at the National Institution for Deaf-Mutes, first as a student, then as a teacher.

Laurent Clerc was one of Jean Massieu's star pupils. Massieu and Clerc would eventually perform together in Sicard's educational exhibitions, which demonstrated the success Sicard had in teaching deaf people. The general public still was amazed that deaf people could learn to read and write, but they seemed fascinated that deaf people could hold philosophical discussions, discuss abstract ideas, and express the whole range of human thoughts and feelings. Sicard's performances were in great demand and he began plans to take his demonstrations to England; but there was also new political turmoil in France. In the Spring of 1815, Napoleon Bonaparte left Elba[4] and marched his way back into power. The king of France had already left the country and so did Sicard, ahead of schedule. He took a group to England for six performances. The group included Massieu, Clerc, and another deaf student. It was in London that Laurent Clerc first met Thomas H. Gallaudet.

Thomas Hopkins Gallaudet was a bright American student. He was born December 10th, 1787. At the age of 14 he had completed his secondary education and was accepted to Yale, where he graduated (at the top of his class) three years later at the age of 17. Within another two years he had earned a master of arts degree from Yale and after

---

[4] Napoleon declared himself the Emperor of France in 1804 and ruled from 1804 until 1814 when he was exiled to the Italian island of Elba. In 1815 he left Elba and regained control of France, but only for three months.

working a while as a salesman, he entered the Andover Theological Seminary at the age of 24. In 1814 he was 26 years old and had just graduated from the Seminary.

During a visit home in 1814, Thomas noticed that one of the neighborhood children, Alice Cogswell, was not being included in the games played by the other children. When Thomas asked his younger brother why she sat alone, the answer was that she was deaf. Thomas worked with Alice and managed to get her to understand some written English. Legend has it that her first word was "hat."

Mason Fitch Cogswell, Alice's father, was thrilled with Gallaudet's efforts. Cogswell had been working toward establishing a school for deaf children in the United States, but he had failed to recruit a teacher to establish a school in New England. Cogswell already owned a copy of L'Epée's 1776 book and was anxious to have someone in New England who could teach his daughter. Otherwise he would eventually have to send Alice overseas to give her the education he wanted for her. Cogswell quickly generated a rough count of the deaf population of New England, determined there were more than enough to justify a school for deaf children, and gathered the elite of Hartford together to reveal his plan. In just one day Cogswell raised enough money for Gallaudet to travel to Europe and learn about deaf education. Thomas Hopkins Gallaudet would soon be on his way to England to begin learning about the methods for educating deaf children. It would be a trip that would change not only his life, but the lives of every generation of American deaf children born since then.

In January of 1815, the War of 1812 was concluding with its final battle: an Andrew Jackson victory in New Orleans. James Madison had returned to the White House (after British troops invaded Washington, DC in August of 1814) and was completing the last half of his second term as President. Francis Scott Key had already written the words to the "Star Spangled Banner" after witnessing the British attempt to take Fort McHenry at Baltimore in 1814. The war had begun in part because the British Navy was frequently capturing American sailors and forcing them to join the British navy in their fight against Napoleon. The major battles of the War of 1812 took place along the Canadian border. New England had been left largely unaffected by armed battles of the war.

By the spring of 1815, Thomas Hopkins Gallaudet had left Connecticut and started his venture in England where he found his own frustration with the British. The national leaders of deaf education in Great Britain were the Braidwoods who had a franchised, for-profit organization that taught deaf children throughout England. The Braidwoods had one member of the family in Cobbs, Virginia. John Braidwood had been teaching Colonel Bolling's two deaf children and would formally open the first American school for deaf children in 1815; however, Braidwood was a drunkard and would not do well in the family business. The Braidwood school in Cobb, Virginia would be shut down by the end of 1817.

The Braidwoods in England welcomed Thomas Hopkins Gallaudet and saw his arrival as an opportunity to expand their franchise further, and more solidly, into the United States; but Gallaudet would only be allowed to learn the Braidwood's "secrets" by contractually agreeing to operate an American school as a franchise of the Braidwood family and sending a portion of the profits to England. Gallaudet refused to sign the contractual agreement but continued to try to negotiate other terms with the Braidwoods.

In March of 1815, during Gallaudet's time in England, Napoleon Bonaparte regained power in France. In May of 1815 Sicard, Massieu, and Clerc had arrived in London and begun a series of performances demonstrating the success of L'Epée's and Sicard's methods. Over several weeks they performed eighteen public performances (twelve more than the number originally planned). These performances included answers to questions from the audience. They were a sensation because they demonstrated that deaf people could actually reason and quite wittily, too.

In July of 1815, Gallaudet was still in England and attended one of the last performances by Sicard's traveling team. Gallaudet was impressed with Sicard, Massieu, and Clerc and wanted to learn more. They invited him to come to Paris since the French political scene was settling down[5]. Sicard and his group went home; but Gallaudet would instead travel to Edinburgh to the original Braidwood school to try to discover the secrets of deaf education there. Finally in February of 1816 he visited the Paris school and began to learn the school's methods from Sicard and Massieu.

Gallaudet's funds were running scarce, having spent a full year in Europe. He knew he had finally found the right place to learn the methods needed to establish an American school, but he no longer had enough time to learn everything he needed to know. Gallaudet asked Sicard's help in finding a knowledgeable assistant to travel to America and establish a school. Sicard recommended Clerc. Clerc had hoped to teach at a school for deaf children in Russia, but that job had been given to a less qualified hearing person instead. Although Clerc was not too anxious to leave Europe, eventually he agreed and traveled with Gallaudet back to Hartford, Connecticut to establish the first *permanent* school for the instruction of deaf children in America. Clerc fully expected that he would at some time return to France.

On June 18, 1816 the ship departed Le Havre, France for the United States. The trip took fifty-two days. Gallaudet had spent his time in the previous four months learning French Sign Language and Clerc had previously been exposed to written English. During the trip each worked with the other to further improve their language fluencies. Upon their arrival in the United States Clerc, 30, and Gallaudet, 28, began a tour of the Northern states to obtain funds for establishing a school. Classes began on April 15th, 1817. A few months later the recently inaugurated fifth U.S. president, James Monroe, would visit the school.

Martha's Vineyard

In the early 1600's English settlers were populating the new world. Among these new settlers were a group of several families from the Kent county area of England. Most of these people traveled together on the same boat and they settled in Southeastern Massachusetts. From there several descendents were among those who moved to Martha's Vineyard, an island off the Southern tip of Massachusetts, below Cape Cod.

Martha's Vineyard was a rather closed community. Transportation between the island and the mainland was too difficult for regular visits back and forth so the people on the island tended to stay close to home and marry other islanders and raise the next generation on the island as their parents had before them. The first recorded incidence of deafness was reported in 1714. The deaf person was Jonathan Lambert, who was born in 1657. Many more incidences of deafness were recorded over the next two centuries. For nearly three centuries there would be a disproportionately high number of deaf people born on the island.

---

[5] Napoleon had just been defeated by the British in Waterloo, Belgium, on June 18th, 1815.

This kind of deafness was inherited. The people from Kent must have had a common ancestor who carried a recessive gene for deafness. As distant descendents married one another on the island, their children had the possibility of being born deaf. As a result, the majority of the population on the island was related in some way with at least one deaf person. This lead to a widespread knowledge of signed language among both the deaf and hearing members of the community.

Signed language was used to help fishermen communicate across large distances of water and even to help them finish dirty jokes when a woman came among their presence. The majority of the community was bilingual in English and Martha's Vineyard Sign Language, and deaf people held the same kinds of jobs that their hearing friends and relatives did. The integration of deaf people among the hearing majority was so great that some residents had difficulty remembering whether well-known community members were deaf or not when they were interviewed by Nora Groce[6] in 1978.

It was from Martha's Vineyard that several deaf students joined the first class of students at the Hartford School. These students, using Martha's Vineyard Sign Language, formed a significant influence on the creation of American Sign Language. As they interacted with their fellow students and their teacher, Laurent Clerc, they contributed portions of their language to the mix that has become ASL as we know it today.

The community of deaf people on Martha's Vineyard began to disappear with improved transportation and a greater number of new families moving to the island, while members of the old, long-standing family lines of Vineyard dwellers moved to the mainland. The last member of the "up-Island" deaf population was Abigail Brewer who died in 1952. Today there is no greater proportion of deafness on the island than anywhere else in the U.S. But there was a time when nearly everyone there knew signed language.

The Connecticut Asylum for the Education and Instruction of Deaf and Dumb Persons

Thomas Gallaudet had gone to England first, rather than France, because of the large chain of private schools for deaf children in England run through the Braidwood family. They kept their methods secret and thus kept a monopoly on their profitable school system. A few deaf children of wealthy Americans had been educated there, but not all succeeded. The school was predominantly oral in its methods, not allowing signed language to be used as a means of instruction.[7]

In 1812, John Braidwood, a grandson of the founder of the British franchise founder, started privately teaching deaf children at the home of Colonel Bolling in Cobbs, Virginia. In 1815, the same year Gallaudet was in Europe to learn educational methods, the first American school for deaf children was established in Cobbs, Virginia. Due to John Braidwood's mismanagement, however, this school would be closed before 1817, recreating the need for a school for deaf children in the United States. The first

---

[6] Groce's 1985 report of her research, "Everyone Here Spoke Sign Language: Hereditary Deafness on Martha's Vineyard" provides most of the data for this chapter.

[7] And yet there is written documentation indicating that some Braidwoods knew and used signed language to communicate with deaf people. Their secret methods may in fact have made some use of signed language.

permanent school for deaf children would be established a few hundred miles to the North, in Connecticut.

The Connecticut Asylum for the Education and Instruction of Deaf and Dumb Persons was established by Laurent Clerc and Thomas Gallaudet. It opened its doors to seven students on **April 15, 1817.** Many of the original students came from Martha's Vineyard off the Massachusetts coast. They had a strong and cohesive signed language there and brought it with them to Hartford. Laurent Clerc knew French Sign Language. When he began teaching his first seven students, he no doubt encountered the signed language of Martha's Vineyard along with a variety of signs used by the other deaf people among themselves in their own hometowns. As the students and their teacher began their lessons they also began to forge the new beginnings of American Sign Language. Clerc incorporated these signs into his own vocabulary and became the model of American Sign Language as we know it today.

One major piece of evidence of this amalgamation is the ASL counting system. Neither wholly American, nor wholly French, it incorporates features of both as evidenced by the use of the American gesture handshapes for the numbers "one," and "two," but using the natural French gesture (and therefore also the French Sign Language handshape) for the number "three." LSF handshapes are used for the numbers 20, 21, and 23 through 30 but not for the number 22, which is based on American gestures.

Under instruction from Laurent Clerc, four of the original seven students would eventually become teachers of even more deaf students. Educators, both deaf and hearing, from across the United States and Canada also visited the school in Hartford, Connecticut. The new American Sign Language, which had only recently been created out of French Sign Language and Old American Sign Language, was learned by every visiting educator. As these educators spread out and established new schools in the United States and in Canada they brought with them the new American Sign Language. This was the essential element needed to ensure the widespread use of American Sign Language in North America.

ASL has a direct, though partial, connection with French Sign Language; it is therefore considered a part of the European Signed Language Family. ASL shares more vocabulary with French Sign Language than with British Sign Language. Yet similarities within the European Signed Language Family allow a certain amount of understanding (and a certain amount of confusion) between users of different European signed languages. The model school program in Hartford, Connecticut established a national center for deaf education in the United States and laid the foundation for a unified American Sign Language, thus preventing the development of a different signed language in each state.

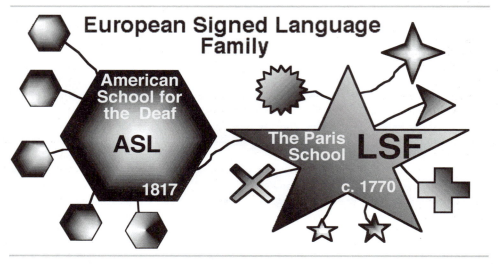

Figure 1.8 – LSF & ASL as Part of the European Signed Language Family

Summary

This Unit presented the history of American Sign Language with its roots in French Sign Language (the language of Laurent Clerc) and the signing of Martha's Vineyard (the majority language of Clerc's first American students). We have learned about three hearing teachers, the Abbé de L'Epée, the Abbé Sicard, and Thomas Hopkins Gallaudet. We have learned about two deaf teachers, Jean Massieu, the first deaf teacher of deaf students in recorded history, and Laurent Clerc, the first deaf teacher of deaf students on the American continent. We have learned about the influence of residential schools for deaf children upon stabilizing and spreading a standardized signed language and how the influences of the Paris school were felt in Hartford and are still obvious today across the United States and in Canada.

Additionally we have seen that this language with its rich history was not acknowledged as a legitimate language for nearly 150 years, even by the deaf people who used it on a daily basis. We have learned about William Stokoe, a hearing man with no native understanding of signed languages, explored and researched American Sign Language and demonstrated that it meets the definition of language. Thanks to Stokoe's efforts, the Deaf community would find pride, rather than shame, in their language. The next Unit will explore the origins of this shame as part of a systematic oppression of the Deaf community.

Timelines in History

The French Revolution began on July 14th, 1789 – 5 months later the Abbé De l'Epée died at the age of 77. In 1790 the Abbé Sicard was selected to run the school. In 1799 Napoleon Bonaparte seized control of the French government. Napoleon's military actions in Europe lead the British navy to make a practice of confiscating American ships and their crews. President Madison declared war on England in 1812. Napoleon was defeated by a European alliance in 1814 and was exiled to the island of Elba. This removed the original conditions of the war of 1812. Napoleon briefly returned to power from March 20th until June 22nd of 1815, having been defeated by the British and Prussian allies at Waterloo, Belgium. T. H. Gallaudet met Sicard and Laurent Clerc in July of 1815 and brought Clerc to America the next year. The Hartford School opened on April 15th, 1817.

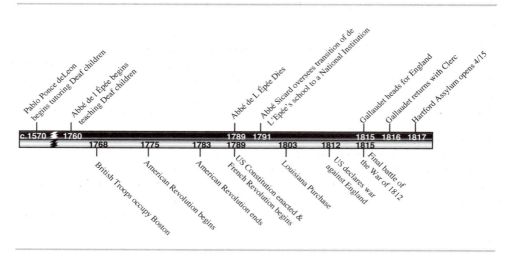

Figure 1.9 – Deaf Education Timeline

Section 1 Review Questions

1) What is the difference between language and communication?

2) What four components are always present in acts of communication?

3) What four additional requirements allow a communication system to be considered a language?

4) What are the three most common communication modalities?

5) What is the difference between language encoding systems and language channels?

6) Who began to conduct research in the 1950s which demonstrated that ASL is a language?

7) What are the four primary parameters of signed languages?

8) What six features provide the evidence that ASL is a language?

9) Why is ASL not a *Universal* language?

10) How is ASL related to French Sign Language?

Section 2 Review Questions

11)   Who was Pablo Ponce De Leon and where did he live?

12)   How did the abbé de L'Epée begin teaching deaf children?

13)   How did Thomas Hopkins Gallaudet become involved in teaching deaf children?

14)   Where did Gallaudet spend the first several months trying to learn about teaching deaf children?

15)   Where did Gallaudet eventually succeed in learning about deaf education?

16)   What year did de L'Epée publish his book?

17)   What war had just concluded before Gallaudet began his journey to learn about deaf education?

18)   Who was Mason Fitch Cogswell?

19)   Who was Thomas Hopkins Gallaudet?

20)   Who were the Braidwoods?

21)   Who was the Abbé de l'Epée?

22)   Who was the Abbé Sicard?

23)   Who was Jean Massieu?

24)   Who was Laurent Clerc?

25)   What European leader's activities lead Sicard, Massieu, & Clerc to flee from France?

26)   How did the Paris school influence signed languages in other European countries?

27)   What kinds of communication were common in Martha's Vineyard in the early 1800's?

28)   Why were there so many deaf people on Martha's Vineyard in the early 1800's?

29)   What date did the American School for the Deaf open?

30)   How did the American School for the Deaf influence signed language in the United States?

Communication, Language & American Sign Language

Baker, C. & Battison R. (eds.) 1980. *Sign Language and the Deaf Community*. Silver Spring, MD: National Association of the Deaf.

Battison R. 1974. Phonological Deletion in American Sign Language. *Sign Language Studies 5*: 1-19.

Battison R. 1978. *Lexical Borrowing in American Sign Language*. Silver Spring, MD: Linstok Press.

Battison R. 1980. Signs Have Parts: A Simple Idea.In Baker, C. & Battison R. (eds.) *Sign Language and the Deaf Community*. Silver Spring, MD: National Association of the Deaf.

Bloom, F. E. & A. Lazerson. 1988. *Brain, Mind, and Behavior: Second Edition*. New York, NY: W. H. Freeman and Company.

Bonvilliam, N. 1993. *Language, Culture, and Communication: The Meaning of Messages (Second Edition)*. Upper Saddle River, NJ: Prentice Hall.

Cerney, B. 1987. "A Reader's Guide to an International Study of Seven Signers." Unpublished Manuscript. Gallaudet University.

Cokely, D., & C. Baker. 1980. *American Sign Language: A Teacher's Resource Text on Grammar and Culture*. Silver Spring, MD: TJ Publishers, Inc.

Costello, E. 1998. *Random House Webster's American Sign Language Dictionary*. New York, NY: Random House.

Crabtree, M. & J. Powers, Eds. *Language Files: Materials for an Introduction to Language*. Columbus Ohio: Ohio State University Press.

Crystal, D. 1987. *The Cambridge Encyclopedia of Language*. New York, NY: Cambridge University Press.

Fant, L. 1983. *The American Sign Language Phrase Book*. Chicago, IL: Contemporary Books, Inc.

Humphries, T., C. Padden, & T.J. O'Rourke. 1994. *A Basic Course in American Sign Language, Second Edition*. Silver Spring, MD: TJ Publishers, Inc.

Klima, E. & U. Bellugi. 1979. *The Signs of Language*. Cambridge, MA: Harvard University Press.

Lentz. E. M., K. Mikos, & C. Smith. 1989. *Signing Naturally: Level 2*. San Diego, CA: Dawn Sign Press.

Mikos, K., C. Smith,, & E. M. Lentz. 2001. *Signing Naturally: Level 3*. San Diego, CA: Dawn Sign Press.

Smith, C., E. M. Lentz & K. Mikos. 1988. *Signing Naturally: Level 1*. San Diego, CA: Dawn Sign Press.

Stokoe, W. 1960. *Sign Language Structure: An Outline of the Visual Communication Systems of the American Deaf*. Burtonsville, MD: Linstok Press.

Stokoe, W. 1965. *The Dictionary of American Sign Language*. Burtonsville, MD: Linstok Press.

Tennant, Richard & Marianne Gluszak Brown. 1998. *The American Sign Language Handshape Dictionary*. Washington,: Clerc Books (Gallaudet University Press).

Valli, C. & C. Lucas. 1995. *Linguistics of American Sign Language: Revised Edition*. Washington, DC: Gallaudet Press.

Woodward, J. 1973. *Implicational Lects on the Deaf Diglossic Continuum*. Unpublished Ph.D. dissertation, Georgetown University.

The Abbé de l'Epée, Sicard, Massieu, Clerc, Gallaudet, & Deaf Education

Carruth, G. 1987. *The Encyclopedia of American Facts & Dates.* New York, NY: Harper and Row.

Eastman, G. 1997 *Sign Me Alice & Laurent Clerc: A Profile.* Dawn Sign Press.

Eriksson, Per. 1998. *The History of Deaf People: A Source Book.* Örebro, Sweden: SIH Läromedel

Gannon, J. 1981. *Deaf Heritage: A Narrative History of Deaf America.* Silver Spring, MD: National Association of the Deaf.

Lane, H. 1984. *When the Mind Hears: A History of the Deaf.* New York: Random House.

Lane, H., R. Hoffmeister, & B. Bahan. 1996. *A Journey into the DEAF-WORLD.* San Diego, CA: Dawn Sign Press.

Neisser, A. 1983. *The Other Side of Silence: Sign Language and the Deaf Community in America.* Washington, DC: Gallaudet University Press.

Padden, C. and T. Humphries. 1988. *Deaf in America: Voices from a Culture.* Cambridge, MA: Harvard University Press.

Sacks, O. 1989. *Seeing Voices: A Journey into the World of the Deaf.* Berkeley, CA: University of California Press.

VanCleve, J. V. & B. A. Crouch. 1989. *A Place of Their Own: Creating the Deaf Community in America.* Washington, DC: Gallaudet University Press.

Martha's Vineyard

Groce, N. E. 1985. *Everyone Here Spoke Sign Language: Hereditary Deafness on Martha's Vineyard.* Cambridge, MA: Harvard University Press.

Kageleiry, Jamie. 1999. *The island that spoke by hand.* Yankee. March: 48-55.

Manualism & the Fight for Self-Empowerment

In Hartford there is only a marker on the site where the first school stood, for one hundred years, on Asylum Avenue.   During the 1920s it moved to its present buildings on fifty green acres in a quiet, lovely neighborhood in West Hartford.   ... Set well back from the road, the main entrance is in a huge red-brick, Georgian-style building with three-story white columns. (A. Neisser, 1982: 114)

In many of these schools, deaf children spend years of their lives among Deaf people — children from Deaf families and Deaf adults who work at the school. Many schools are staffed to some extent by Deaf people who graduated from the same school or another one like it. For these deaf children, the most significant aspect of residential life is the dormitory. In the dormitories, away from the structured control of the classroom, deaf children are introduced to the social life of Deaf people. In the informal dormitory environment children learn not only sign language but the content of the culture. In this way, the schools become hubs of the communities that surround them, preserving for the next generation the culture of earlier generations. (C. Padden & T. Humphries, 1988:6)

The stunning architecture of many residential schools for deaf children represents a significant symbol of pride and heritage to the deaf community. The schools are often grand structures that suggest a certain historic permanence to the Deaf community. Such architecture provides historic landmarks that Deaf people will often seek out when they travel across the country. Graduates return with pride to these symbols of their language and culture.

While the residential schools were the focal point for language policy, as dictated by hearing educators, they managed to maintain the rich heritage that had begun in 1817 with Laurent Clerc and Thomas Hopkins Gallaudet. Even when signed languages were officially banned from every residential school, the schools still provided the essential link of maintaining language and culture within the deaf community as the deaf children and adults signed in secret.

This Unit reviews the battles between the use of signed languages for teaching deaf children and the exclusion of signed languages from the instruction of deaf children. You will discover the proponents of each view and how this struggle still continues to this day. You will also investigate some other areas shared by the deaf and hearing communities.

Look for the answers to the following questions as you read:

1) How are Language and Culture interconnected?

2) How can labels and language policy contribute to oppression?

3) Why would members of a minority "Internalize" the oppression of the majority?

4) Who were the leading proponents of the use of signs for instructing deaf people?

5) What political/professional organizations were established to promote this view?

6) What media resources did Deaf people use to discuss goals and plan the actions of the community?

7) What new technologies were used by proponents of the use of signs?

8) Who were the leading proponents of the exclusion of signs from deaf schools?

9) What political/professional organizations were established to promote this view?

10) What new technologies played an associated role (and funding) to the oralists?

11) What is paternalism and how does the Deaf community respond?

Section 1 –Language, Culture & Oppression
Language and Culture

College-level courses that attempt to teach a language will also expose students to the culture or cultures related to the language. Spanish texts may discuss Spanish culture, Mexican culture, and/or a variety of Latin American cultures. Likewise, any investigation of a culture must recognize the language or languages used by members of the culture. Where there is language, there is culture; and where there is culture, there is language. The two concepts are completely intertwined based on the first two parts of the definition of language: Languages are systems of creating symbols that are shared by a community of users. The community determines what the symbols and systems will be. The community will therefore reflect its values through language and the language will be used to discuss and pass on the tradition of those values to the next generation.

Sociolinguistics is the study of language and the ways it is really used by its communities. While it is possible to analyze grammatical patterns in isolation or to explain the patterns of social customs, sociolinguistics provides the whole picture of meaningful language use within context. A quick example of this is to compare the following two sentences: 1) "Its cold in here" and 2) "Please turn the heat up". While it is certainly possible to say both sentences together, it is also possible for sentence #1 to produce the effect of sentence #2. People can understand a simple comment about temperature – "It's cold in here" – to mean "Please turn the heat up."

Two competing views have been presented in a sort of "which came first?" philosophical argument: 1) either language influences the culture (the "Sapir-Whorf" hypothesis) or 2) culture influences language (Dell Hymes' counter-hypothesis). The most obvious resolution to this debate is "Why can't it be both?" It seems obvious that as the culture changes new words are developed (Space-shuttle, e-mail, jet-ski) and that words such as "new" and "improved" can influence our thought, or our cultural perspective.[8]

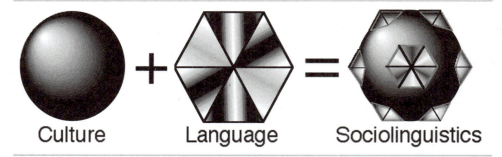

Culture   Language   Sociolinguistics

Figure 2.1 - Language & Culture

---

[8] Even though we have no idea what is "new" or "improved" about a product, we are tempted by these words to think that one box of a product is better than the one sitting next to it just because of these words.

The Power of Labels

One consideration to the overlap of Language and Culture is the labels used to identify a community. The Deaf community uses the word "Deaf" as a means of positive identity. There is no embarrassment or desire to hide this identity among members of the Deaf community. Other labels have emerged over time, from the archaic (and now insulting) "Deaf and Dumb" to the more common "Hearing-Impaired". The word "Dumb" used to mean *silent*; but over time the label has changed to become an indication of limited intelligence, thus an insult to the Deaf community. The label "Hearing-Impaired", while seemingly generic and shorter than the phrase "Deaf & Hard of Hearing", carries the stigma of identifying people by what they are not – their hearing is impaired. The use of this label reveals a medical perspective of deafness rather than a cultural view of the Deaf community.

Some other aspects of the use of labels inside and outside of a group is the use of capital letters. You may have noticed that when this text refers to the Deaf community, the word "Deaf" is capitalized. When talking about only the audiological condition of deafness, however, the word is not capitalized. As you read further, pay attention to the names of organizations founded and run by Deaf people. You will notice that they consistently use the label "Deaf" rather than "Hearing-Impaired".

Internalized Oppression

Oppression is not limited to the deaf experience. Oppression occurs where a majority asserts control over a minority, or even when a controlling minority asserts control over a majority. During colonial empire building by England, France, Portugal, and Spain the natives of the conquered territories were considered savage and uncivilized simply because they had their own cultures and their own success at how they lived and governed themselves. Harlan Lane draws comparisons of the oppression of colonized people with the oppression of deaf people in his book Mask of Benevolence:

> The Belgian colonizers have written of Burundians: The natives are children... superficial, frivolous, fickle. The chiefs are suspicious, cunning and lazy." As long as white men had charge of the affairs of the Africans, this was the condescending and demeaning conception of them that reigned in government.
>
> ...
>
> And indeed, a reputed authority on deafness writes in an American psychiatry journal: "Suspiciousness, paranoid symptomatology, impulsiveness, aggressiveness have been reported as typical of deaf adults... More recent reports tend to confirm these judgments." Here is another expert's published perception of deaf people: "The deaf are more impulsive and aggressive than the hearing, they have deficiencies in language skills, their intellectual development is delayed..." Likewise, a summary of published research on the "psychology of the deaf" that is frequently cited in the United States finds "rigidity, emotional immaturity, social ineptness." (Harlan Lane, 1992, pp 33-35)

The point that Lane makes by citing all of these examples is that they are labels given by outsiders who know little about the people of Burundi or the deaf community and see them only as an impaired population, less than wholly human, and needy of professional help. This is the normal behavior of oppressors, to define the oppressed as being deficient, thus justifying the oppressor's role as one providing balance.

Oralists found that they could gain significant power and financial benefits if they convinced the parents of deaf children that only they held the keys to the deaf child's success. The only way to do this was to eliminate the self-success of the deaf community. Where deaf teachers had established and managed their own schools for decades in the United States, the oralists were able to play upon the fear of the unknown and the visible differences between signed and spoken languages to assert power over these schools, force the deaf teachers to retire (because they could hardly be good models of speech) and completely abolish the use of signed languages not only in the schools but in public as well.

As oralism became the standard and accepted way to educate deaf children it began to erode the progress and pride of the deaf community. Deaf children were taught that speech was good and signing was bad. As these deaf children became deaf adults they believed it was taboo to use signs or even gestures in public. They had internalized the oppression of their teachers and carried forth their oppressors' beliefs into their own adult lives. Deaf people were ashamed to sign in public. Many even refused to sign in front of their own children. By the time William Stokoe decided to investigate the possibility that signing was actually a language, the deaf teachers at Gallaudet ridiculed him for wasting his time on such a silly notion. They had internalized the belief that their own native language was not a legitimate language and even worked to impede his progress in demonstrating otherwise.

Section 2 – Manualism Versus Oralism
The New England Gallaudet Association
By 1850 the American Asylum in Hartford had become a central point for drawing students from across the United States. Although the New York state school had opened in 1818, the Hartford School was the one that provided education for deaf students in Massachusetts, New Hampshire, Vermont, Maine, Rhode Island, Connecticut, South Carolina and Georgia. With the majority of graduates from Hartford remaining in New England it was not difficult for alumni members to remain in close contact with each other.

The New England Gallaudet Association originally was founded as a response to the death of Thomas Hopkins Gallaudet in 1851. Hartford Alum, Thomas Brown of New Hampshire organized a meeting in Vermont that brought together graduates of the school. The purpose of the meeting was to begin collecting funds and establish a monument to honor Gallaudet. Laurent Clerc was elected as the president of the Gallaudet Monument Association. The same meeting also suggested a permanent organization to honor Gallaudet's memory be established and William Chamberlain was given the duty of drafting a constitution for the organization. The first meeting of the NEGA was in March of 1854.

Throughout New England there were small networks of deaf people. But even with the creation of the New England Gallaudet Association, communication in the deaf community relied on print media to reach its widely dispersed audience. While each local residential school often had its own school newspaper, the main mechanism for keeping a national deaf community in contact was the American Annals of the Deaf.

The American Annals of the Deaf
The American Annals of the Deaf was first published at the Hartford School in 1847. It served as the main medium for intellectual discussion about the advancement of Deaf people. One of the hot topics discussed in the 1850s was the notion of creating a Deaf territory or state. John Flournoy, a graduate of the Hartford school proposed that given the difficulties that deaf people experienced as minority members of their communities, it would make sense for them to migrate west and establish their own territory, governed by and for themselves. While many people responded favorably to the idea, it was quickly pointed out that one major problem would be the children of the deaf settlers, who would statistically be overwhelmingly hearing. Would they be forced to leave when they became adults? The notion did not go further than being a topic of discussion. Another issue that John Flournoy strongly advocated was a deaf college. In this effort he was joined by another Hartford graduate, John Carlin. Edward Miner Gallaudet and Amos Kendall would eventually establish what is now Gallaudet University with support generated through the letters published in the American Annals. John Carlin received the first honorary degree awarded at Gallaudet, a Masters of Arts, in 1864

The American Annals of the Deaf continues now primarily as the official joint publication of the Convention of American Instructors of the Deaf (founded in 1850, also in Hartford) and the Conference of Educational Administrators of Schools and Programs for the Deaf (founded in 1868). Its research articles have explored oral education, manual education, cultural issues and more mundane issues of school administration. Its 150th anniversary issue in 1997 republished many articles from its inaugural year, resulting in the seeming impossibility of Edward Miner Gallaudet and John Carlin receiving publication credits in the year 1997.

Edward Miner Gallaudet, the Columbia Institution for the Instruction of the Deaf and Dumb, and the National Deaf-Mute College

Thomas Hopkins Gallaudet was born in 1787. In 1820, at the age of 33, he met his future wife, Sophia Fowler while teaching at the American Asylum in Hartford. She was deaf and was a student at the school. After they married, they raised a large family of bilingual children (using ASL and English). When Thomas Hopkins Gallaudet's eighth and last child, Edward Miner Gallaudet, was born in 1837, Thomas had already retired from the American Asylum in Connecticut. Fourteen years later, Thomas H. Gallaudet died on September 10th, 1851.

Thomas Gallaudet, the first child born to Thomas and Sophia Gallaudet, followed his parents' footsteps by working with the deaf community. In 1850, one year before his father died, Thomas began a Sunday school class for deaf people at St. Stephens Episcopal Church in New York City. Soon afterward he resigned from his teaching position at the New York Institute for the Deaf and in 1851 he became an ordained priest in the Episcopal church. Reverend Thomas Gallaudet founded the first church in the United States that was designed exclusively for deaf people. Only one of Thomas Gallaudet's seven siblings, Edward, also pursued a life's work with the deaf community.

Amos Kendall was a politically connected postmaster general who had collaborated with Samuel Morse in the first demonstration of the use of telegraphy that included the running of a cable from Washington, DC to Baltimore, Maryland (45 miles away). The cable crossed over part of Kendall's property that is now Gallaudet University. Morse's wife was deaf and therefore Kendall had some knowledge of the needs for visual communication among deaf people. In 1856, Amos Kendall established a small school for the instruction of deaf and blind children on two acres of his own estate in North East Washington, DC.

The first person that Kendall hired to teach the children ran off with the money and left the children to the care of the cook. Kendall decided to find the best replacement he could so in 1857 he hired the young Edward Miner Gallaudet (all of twenty years old at the time) to become the superintendent. Because of Edward's youth, Edward's deaf mother, Sophia Fowler Gallaudet, became part of the package deal as an advisor to Edward. That year (1857) the school was incorporated by the U.S. Congress as the Columbia Institution for the Instruction of the Deaf and Dumb and the Blind.

The school began with four deaf children and four blind children. Edward sought to build the school into a college for deaf people. In 1864, he succeeded (with significant help from Kendall's political connections) in getting the U.S. Congress to pass a bill allowing the school to confer college degrees. Abraham Lincoln signed the bill on April 8, 1864 and so began the National Deaf Mute College. Blind students were transferred to a school in Maryland and the focus of the education shifted fully to deaf people. Edward Miner Gallaudet (EMG) became the first president of the college.

At first the college only accepted men, but by 1887 deaf women were admitted to the college. Four years later, in 1891, the college began teaching people to become teachers of deaf children. In 1894 the Collegiate Division (but not the entire institution) was renamed Gallaudet College to honor Thomas H. Gallaudet. Edward Miner Gallaudet was a major proponent for the use of signed language in the education of deaf people. He resigned in 1910, after 46 years as president. He died in Hartford, Connecticut in 1917. In 1954 the United States Congress would officially change the name of the entire Institution to Gallaudet College and would change it again in 1986 to Gallaudet University.[9]

Alexander Graham Bell and the American Association to Promote the Teaching of Speech to the Deaf

When Alexander Graham Bell invented the telephone, legend says, he was actually trying to perfect a device to help deaf people hear better. The telephone and hearing aid are related in that they electronically amplify sounds. Bell's interest in deaf people stemmed from his parents. Alexander Melville Bell taught speech and articulation of sounds to deaf people. He had married a deaf woman who used oral means of communication. When Alexander Graham Bell sought a wife, he too chose a deaf woman who did not use signed language to communicate: Mabel Hubbard.

Alexander Graham Bell proposed that oral education was the best means for teaching deaf children. He saw the education of deaf children as a way of restoring deaf children to the society at large. He had a great influence upon the spread of oral schools in this country. He worked extensively with schools in Madison and Milwaukee, Wisconsin to establish day school programs for deaf children. Bell believed that one significant problem with deaf education was that it congregated deaf people together where they would be even more tempted to communicate manually rather than orally. By establishing day school programs within normal educational settings, Bell hoped to increase the chances that deaf children would communicate via speechreading and speech production.

Bell fell in love with a deaf speech student of his, Mabel Hubbard. Her father was Gardiner Greene Hubbard, a patent attorney, whose efforts are the primary reason that Bell was given the patent for telephone technology.[10] Hubbard was also a co-founder of the Clarke School, an oral school for deaf children in Massachusetts. With prize money for his invention of the telephone, Bell established the Volta Bureau as an organization for the collection and dissemination of knowledge about deafness. The Volta Bureau's headquarters is still running today in Georgetown, Washington, DC. Out of the Volta Bureau, Bell created the American Association to Promote the Teaching of Speech to the Deaf, now called the Alexander Graham Bell Association.

In 1883, Bell addressed the National Academy of Science in New Haven, Connecticut. His topic was "Upon the Formation of a Deaf Variety of the Human Race." Bell had seen the high incidence of deafness on Martha's Vineyard. He noticed that certain children attending the American School for the Deaf in Hartford, Connecticut and at the residential school in Illinois had the same surnames as classes in the previous generation. Bell suspected that educating deaf people in residential schools was causing them to limit their interaction with the rest of society. He believed that residential schools which used signing would sharply increase the number of deaf marriages and

---

[9] Each change in name required an act of congress and the signature of the President. To this day, Gallaudet diplomas bear the signature of the sitting US president at the time of each graduation.
[10] Therefore, if you plan to invent anything of value, be sure you have a good patent attorney in the family!

eventually lead to the creation of a deaf race of people. While some deafness is hereditary (perhaps as much as 10%) the majority of deafness occurs accidentally. But Bell did not know this and even attempted to have Congress make it illegal for deaf people to marry one another in this country.

In fact the general statistics indicate that 90% of deaf children have hearing parents. When deaf children grow up and have children of their own, 90% of them end up having hearing children. There is no more than a 10% link of multi-generational deafness. With the majority of deaf children being born to hearing parents, some people have suggested (jokingly) that the best way to reduce the numbers of deaf children being born would be to prohibit *hearing people* from having children.

The National Association of the Deaf

The first meeting of the National Association of the Deaf (NAD) took place in Cincinnati, Ohio in August of 1880. In attendance were deaf teachers, deaf school principals, deaf businessmen and other deaf people. These members of the Deaf community had all been educated in a school system barely 60 years old in the United States. They had succeeded under what was called "manual" education, that is, through the use of a natural signed language: American Sign Language. Three deaf men are credited with the founding of the NAD: Edmund Booth, Robert P. McGregor, and Edwin A. Hodgson. These people formed the NAD to protect their own rights as deaf people and to promote an increased awareness and acceptance of deaf people. They elected a deaf man, Robert P. McGregor of Ohio, as their first president. The NAD has consistently remained a deaf-controlled organization since that time. On their 100th anniversary in 1980 the NAD returned to Cincinnati for their biennial convention and at that time they installed Gertrude Galloway as their first female president.

Established in 1880, the NAD is older than the National Association for the Advancement of Colored People (NAACP) and older than most other special-interest group advocacy organizations. The need for a national organization serving deaf people had been discussed off and on for thirty years. There were other organizations serving the needs of deaf people prior to this time, such as the New England Gallaudet Association of the Deaf, which had been established in 1853; but there was no national organization prior to 1880.

Rutherford B. Hayes was president of the United States in 1880, which was also the year that Helen Keller was born. Laurent Clerc had died eleven years previously – in 1869; but there were now thirty-eight schools for deaf children and eight of them had been founded by deaf people, many of whom had been taught by Clerc in Hartford. The 1880 U.S. census would record 51,155,783 people, of whom 33,878 people were identified as being "deaf-mute." The deaf people who gathered in Cincinnati came from 21 of the 38 states which the U.S. had so far. As it happened, the geographic center of the U.S. population that year was only eight miles west and south of Cincinnati.

The Deaf people who gathered were concerned about the changes being made in deaf education. There had already begun a movement in the United States to eliminate the use of signed language in deaf education and replace it with oral methodology. In addition, deaf people were concerned about job training needs and general discrimination issues. They realized that they were the people best equipped to help themselves. The first convention resolved "... to bring the Deaf of the different sections of the United States in close contact and to deliberate on the needs of the deaf as a class. We have interests peculiar to ourselves which can be taken care of by ourselves."

One of the early issues taken on by the National Association of the Deaf was how to deal with "Deaf Peddlers." Deaf peddlers were people who used their deafness, and the public's pity for deaf people, as a means of making money. Typically a deaf peddler sells small cards with the Manual Alphabet on one side and some plea for assistance on the other side. The NAD clearly stated a position against all people who participated in this kind of activity (not all deaf peddlers were deaf!) The primary reason that the NAD had such a strong disfavor of this kind of activity was that it sent the wrong message to the general public. The NAD already knew that most hearing people did not know much about the deaf community or signed languages. While the NAD was working to improve the lives of deaf people nationwide, it faced discrimination based on low expectations; the public did not understand what deaf people could do and simply assumed that most deaf people could not lead productive lives. Deaf peddlers fostered this myth because they were the only contact that many hearing people ever had with deaf people. The NAD worked diligently to discourage any deaf or hearing person from peddling deafness.

The National Association of the Deaf has national conventions every two years. National conventions are held in even-numbered years and usually are held during the first week of July. State Chapters have their state conventions in odd-numbered years. Delegates from state affiliates attend the national business meetings while thousands of other deaf people and members of the deaf community make new friends, attend educational training sessions, and enjoy the atmosphere of a major deaf event.

In 1967 the NAD was awarded a grant to establish pilot sign language courses. The NAD set up the Communicative Skills Program and hired Terrance O'Rourke, a deaf teacher, as its director. In 1972 the Graduate School at New York University began accepting American Sign Language for its language requirements; and at least 38 other colleges offered credited courses in some form of manual communication. In 1975 the NAD established the Sign Instructors Guidance Network (SIGN), which would later become the American Sign Language Teacher's Association (ASLTA). The ASLTA certifies teachers of American Sign Language and coordinates conferences for ASL teachers.

Over the years the NAD has worked on national legislation including the Television Decoder Circuitry Act and the Americans with Disabilities Act (both of 1990). The NAD worked closely with the student leaders of the Deaf President Now movement to help ensure victory. The NAD also has coordinated efforts to protest films in which deaf characters are portrayed by hearing actors rather than by deaf actors. Their most recent efforts have included working with the FCC to establish more comprehensive requirements for television broadcasts to be closed captioned.

While the NAD works primarily on issues that have a national impact, their state chapters focus on issues facing state legislatures from funding residential schools to lobbying for legislation that promotes effective and ethical interpreting services within each state. Many state affiliates of the NAD also have sub-affiliates in various cities. Through this network of affiliates the Deaf community has worked together to fight for their own needs at local, state, and national levels.

The International Convention of Instructors of the Deaf in Milan, Italy

The International Congress for the Improvement of the Condition of Deaf-Mutes was held at the end of September in Paris, France in 1878 and attended by only twenty-seven people. No American educators attended (some Americans received their invitations received after the conference had already taken place). One of the resolutions from this meeting revealed the philosophical leanings of the leading educators of deaf children in Europe:

> The Congress, after mature deliberation, is of the opinion that, while the use of signs with all deaf-mutes should be retained as an aid in instruction and as the first means of communication between teacher and pupil, preference should be given to the method of articulation and lipreading, which has for its purpose the restoration of the deaf-mute to society – a preference which is further justified by the use generally made of this method in all the nations of Europe and even in America. (Fay, 1879: 57)

The next conference was to take place in Como, Italy in 1881, however changes were made both in the year (to 1880) and the location (to Milan) of the meeting. This time the Americans had sufficient notice to attend.

Oral Education had its formal founding by Samuel Heinicke around the year 1755 when he established an oral school in Germany. This was the same year that Charles Abbé de L'Epee began teaching using the "manual" method in Paris. Thus, each approach to teaching deaf children has an equally long heritage. De L'Epee (and later, Sicard) openly shared their methodology and it spread widely across Europe; but it still required people to travel to directly learn the method (for the most part, this meant learning French Sign Language). Heinicke's methods, although considered deficient by deaf people, did not require the instructor to learn a new language.

In early September of 1880, only one month after the NAD held its founding meeting, an International Convention of Instructors of the Deaf took place in Milan, Italy. The overwhelming majority of people attending the convention were Italian (87 people), followed by a large contingent of French (56 people). Of the remaining 21 people, eight were Englishmen, five were Americans, and the rest from various countries. Only the Americans had been formally elected to represent the deaf education system of their country. The Americans had been elected at a meeting of educators of the deaf which represented the educators of over 6,000 students at 51 schools in the United States. The number of students represented by all of the remaining 159 conference attendees was less than the number represented by just the five American delegates. Edward Miner Gallaudet and his brother, Thomas, were members of the American delegation, as were James Denison, professor at the National Deaf-Mute College; Isaac Lewis Peet, principal of the New York School for the Deaf; and C.A. Stoddard.

The Italians dominated the convention and used it as a means to establish oral educational methods as the predominant way for educating deaf children: not only in their own country, but worldwide. The group excluded deaf participants by establishing a rule that those who could not hear the source language of the conference had to successfully lip-read the proceedings (because the accuracy of an interpreter could not be assured). One deaf person met this requirement; the others did not (including James Denison, the one deaf member of the American delegation). Each remaining person who paid the conference fee had one vote. Even though the Americans represented more schools and more deaf students than all the remaining "delegates" combined, they only had the voting force of four out of over 150 votes.

The oralists submitted a resolution stating that the conference agreed that the only effective way to educate deaf children was the pure oral method. The oralists won, proclaiming a "unanimous victory," despite the fact that the four American votes and an additional British vote had been cast against the resolution. Edward Miner Gallaudet reported the resolution of the convention in the American Annals of the Deaf as follows:

> The Convention, considering the incontestable superiority of speech over signs, (a) for restoring deaf-mutes to social life, and (b) for giving them greater facility of language, declares that the method of articulation should have the preference over that of signs in instruction in education of the deaf and dumb.
>
> Considering that the simultaneous use of signs and speech has the disadvantage of injuring speech and lipreading and precision of ideas, the Convention declares that the oral method ought to be preferred. (E. Gallaudet, 1881: 12)

The effect was almost immediate worldwide. Every school for deaf children that had not previously changed to oral methods would change within the next few decades. Sign language was forbidden in schools serving deaf children. Children began to receive punishment, including striking the hands with rulers or tying them behind the students' backs, if they used their hands to communicate. Deaf adults no longer freely used signed language in public. The effect of the Milan Conference was to proclaim signed languages as dangerous and counter-effective in the task of educating deaf children. All efforts in deaf education shifted from teaching deaf children a wide variety of academic subjects to primarily trying to teach them to speak and lipread.

This method of teaching by oral means only had already been introduced in America in 1864 when Bernard Engelsman came to New York City from the Vienna oral school. On March 1, 1867 his growing school was moved to 134 West 27th Street and was renamed as the Lexington School. That same year saw the opening of the second oral-only school, the Clarke School of Northampton, Massachusetts. Gardiner Greene Hubbard began looking for funding from the state of Massachusetts in 1864 but was not able to receive any. He started a small school to help his daughter Mabel, who had become deaf at the age of five. John Clarke, inspired by a deaf child named Theresa Dudley, had promised $50,000 for the purpose of building a school in Northampton. Later Hubbard found out about Clarke's funding and together they established the Clarke School which opened in October of 1867.

Oral-only teaching methodologies were a rarity in America prior to 1880. After the Milan Conference, however, oralism moved toward replacing manualism in deaf schools. The Pennsylvania School for the Deaf in Philadelphia was the first major residential school to convert from manualism to pure-oralism in 1892. Nebraska passed legislation in 1911 requiring the oral method in its deaf schools. The effect of the Milan Conference was so complete that by 1930 not one residential school for deaf children in the world used sign language for any part of instruction. The only place that used sign language for education was Gallaudet College and even there the pressure was significant to avoid the use of signs where possible.

The Preservation of the Sign Language

In 1913 the National Association of the Deaf committed $5,000 to the making of films intended to guarantee that signed language would survive the Oralist movement. The European schools for deaf children had all quickly become oral-only environments soon after the Milan Conference. The schools in the United States were slower to adopt the oral-only methods but by 1913, only thirty-three years after the Milan conference, the majority of American schools for deaf children had already made the change and it was clear that the trend was not stopping soon.

George Veditz graduated from the Maryland School for the Deaf and was a professional educator. Serving as the seventh president of the National Association of the Deaf, he was filmed in 1913 stating the position of the NAD as representative of the American Deaf community. This eleven-minute, rough black and white film was entitled simply "The Preservation of the Sign Language". It sounds an alarm against the rapid progress of oralist oppression by those who would seek personal advantage and ignore the wishes and experience of the Deaf community. A translation of its entire contents follows:

> Friends and fellow deaf-mutes. The Deaf people of France love de L'Epée and annually upon the occasion of his birthday they gather together at banquets and other festivities to offer their heartfelt appreciation of his efforts on this earth. They travel to his burial site in Versailles to lay flowers and wreaths upon his grave in order to show their respect for his memory. They love him because he was their first teacher; but they love him even more because he was the grandfather and creator of their beautiful signed language.

> For the past thirty-three years the French deaf have watched with eyes filled with tears and with hearts broken in two as their beautiful language of signs has been forcefully taken from their schools. During these past thirty-three years they have endeavored and struggled to regain the use of their signed language in their schools; but for all of those thirty-three years the teachers in these schools have ignored their pleas. Meanwhile these teachers are perfectly willing to listen to people who believe they know all there is to know about teaching deaf people but in fact know nothing of the deaf community, their thoughts, spirit, wants or needs.

> The same is true in Germany. The German Deaf community, as well as the French Deaf community, look to us American Deaf people with envious eyes. They look upon us much like a shackled prisoner looks upon free men casually strolling beyond the confines of the prisoner's bars. They freely admit that the American Deaf community is superior in thought, in learning, and in their success in the world. They freely admit that the American Deaf community is superior in these things for a single reason: we are still allowed to use our beautiful signed language in our schools. They see their own abilities as inferior for a similar reason: they must follow strictly oral methods of education in their schools, without fingerspelling, without the use of signs.

> We American Deaf people are quickly approaching similarly foul times for our own schools. False prophets have come forth proclaiming that our methods for teaching deaf children are in error. These men are trying to teach, and make people believe, that the oral method is the one true and best method for teaching deaf children; but we American Deaf people know, as do the French Deaf people and the German Deaf people, that the oral method is the poorest of all possible methods.

> Our beautiful signed language is beginning to show the results of their efforts. They have strived to remove our signed language from our classrooms,

from our churches, and indeed from the face of the earth. We are now seeing detrimental effects upon our signed language. Renowned masters of our language such as the Peets, the Dudleys, the Elys, and the Ballards are disappearing without replacement. These men inspired us through their eloquent signed orations.

However, we still have many great signed language orators among us including Edward Miner Gallaudet, who learned signs from his father, Thomas Hopkins Gallaudet. And there are others such as Dr. John B. Hotchkiss, Dr. Edward Allen Fay, and Robert P. McGregor who are still among us today. We wish to preserve a record of their performances for the coming generations. There are so many men still alive who learned their signs from such master orators. We know of but one medium with which we would be able to preserve their performances: moving picture films.

Already our National Association of the Deaf has gathered together a fund of five thousand dollars for this purpose. We now have films of Edward Miner Gallaudet, of Fay, of Hotchkiss, and of McGregor and numerous others

I am only sorry that we do not have twenty thousand dollars for we could surely make use of all of such an amount. We could document rallies in signs, sermons in signs, lectures in signs. We would not be limited to documenting our American signs but would be able to document the signs of deaf people in Germany, in England, in France and in Italy. We must provide documentation and preservation via motion picture films. We will see in a mere fifty years that these recordings will indeed have become priceless.

A *race of pariahs* have already taken control of many of our American schools. They themselves do not understand sign language because they themselves cannot communicate through signs. They proclaim that signing is wasteful and does nothing to help deaf people. *As enemies of the sign language; they are enemies of the true welfare of the deaf.* We have a responsibility to pass our signed language on to the next generation

As long as we have Deaf people on this Earth, there will be signed languages; and as long as we have our films we can preserve our beautiful signed language. We must hope that we all will continue to cherish and protect our beautiful signed language as the noblest gift that God has given to deaf people. (George Veditz, 1913; translation by Brian Cerney)

The project successfully recorded at least six other well-regarded signers including orations by E.M. Gallaudet, E.A. Fay, J.B. Hotchkiss, R.P. McGregor, A. Draper and G. Dougherty. These films survive today in the Archives of Gallaudet University and have been transferred to videotape.

Veditz' warning was accurate. By 1930, less than seventeen years after he recorded the message above, not a single pre-college classroom permitted the use of signs or even gesture as a part of the education of deaf children. The only place in the world that still permitted the overt use of signing was Gallaudet College. In less than fifty years the proclamations of the Milan Conference had undone the progress of the previous century of deaf education and it would be several more decades before signing of any form was again allowed in classrooms for deaf children.

Summary

This Unit presented the opposing sides of Manualism and Oralism. We have learned about Edward Miner Gallaudet and George Veditz, two leading advocates for the advancement of deaf people and the free use of their native language - American Sign Language. We have learned about Alexander Graham Bell and the oralist movement, which sought to eliminate the use of signing and deaf leadership under the guise of "helping" deaf children. We have learned about the powerful results of the Milan Conference in 1880 which eventually led to the complete removal of sign language from all of deaf education world-wide, save for the classrooms of Gallaudet College; and we have learned about the National Association of the Deaf which stood in the path of the oralists' progress to eradicate signed language, made significant efforts to document and preserve the language, and spoke in defense of the right for deaf people to use their own native language. Finally, we have been exposed to the concept of oppression through language policy and the phenomenon known as "internalized oppression."

Timelines in History

As the United States moved from a largely agricultural society into a more industrial one the Deaf community was becoming empowered through the residential schools which were being founded in various states by graduates of the Hartford school and by educators who visited the school and modeled new schools after it. Amos Kendall, wealthy from his association with Samuel Morse, established a school for deaf children in Washington, DC and brought Edward Miner Gallaudet from Hartford down to DC to run the school. E. M. Gallaudet, in turn, brought the best teachers from Hartford and in less than ten years Congress and president Lincoln authorized the school to award college degrees. Only sixteen years later a group of deaf education leaders in Europe began the process of banning the use of signed languages in schools for deaf children. The National Association of the Deaf (founded the same year as the Milan Conference) led by its president, George Veditz, was not able to stop the spread of oralism and by the 1930s signed language had been banned in every American school except for Gallaudet College.

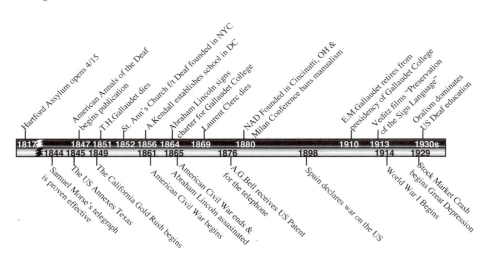

Section 1 Review Questions

1)   What is the relationship between language and culture?

2)   What is the "Sapir-Whorf" hypothesis of the relationship between language and culture?

3)   Who proposed the view contrasting Sapir-Whorf?

4)   What are some of the labels that are found to be insulting by members of the Deaf community.

5)   What is internalized oppression?

6)   How did Deaf people at Gallaudet exhibit internalized oppression regarding Stokoe's research?

Section Two Review Questions

7)   What reason brought the New England Gallaudet Association together?

8)   Where were the American Annals of the Deaf first published?

9)   Who was Amos Kendall and what influence did he have on higher education for Deaf people?

10)   How did Samuel Morse and the telegraph have any impact on Deaf history?

11)   What year saw both the Milan Conference and foundation of the NAD?

12)   What goals and purposes were pursued by the National Association of the Deaf?

13)   What goals and purposes were pursued by the members of the Milan Conference?

14)   Which of these two gatherings were controlled and managed by Deaf people?

15)   What restrictions were placed on deaf people who attended the Milan Conference?

16)   What was the nearly immediate result of the Milan Conference in Europe?

17)   Who funded "The Preservation of the Sign Language"?

18)   What year was "The Preservation of the Sign Language" produced?

19)   Identify at least four people who participated in "The Preservation of the Sign Language" project.

20)   Identify at least two different presidents of the NAD.

21)   What are "deaf peddlers?"

22)   What position was held by the NAD regarding Deaf peddlers?

23)   Which side of the oral/manual debate were each of the following people:

        Alexander Graham Bell

        Edward Miner Gallaudet

        George Veditz

        Gardiner Greene Hubbard

        Robert P. McGregor

        Edward Allen Fay

Organizations Serving Deaf People

Gallaudet, E. M. 1983. *History of the College for the Deaf: 1857 - 1907*. Washington, DC: Gallaudet College Press.

Gannon, J. 1981. *Deaf Heritage: A Narrative History of Deaf America*. Silver Spring, MD: National Association of the Deaf.

Lane, H., R. Hoffmeister, & B. Bahan. 1996. *A Journey into the DEAF-WORLD*. San Diego, CA: Dawn Sign Press.

Padden, C. and T. Humphries. 1988. *Deaf in America: Voices from a Culture*. Cambridge, MA: Harvard University Press.

VanCleve, J. V. & B. A. Crouch. 1989. *A Place of Their Own: Creating the Deaf Community in America*. Washington, DC: Gallaudet University Press.

Wilcox, S., Ed. 1992. *American Deaf Culture: An Anthology*. Burtonsville, MD: Linstok Press.

Manualism versus Oralism

Brill, R. 1984. *International Congress on education of the Deaf: An Analytical History 1878 - 1980*. Washington, DC: Gallaudet College Press.

Gallaudet, E. M. 1881. Resolutions of the Milan convention. *American Annals of the Deaf, 26*.

Lane, H. 1984. *When the Mind Hears: A History of the Deaf*. New York: Random House.

Lane, H. 1992. *The Mask of Benevolence: Disabling the Deaf Community*. New York: Alfred A. Knopf.

Neisser, A. 1983. *The Other Side of Silence: Sign Language and the Deaf Community in America*. Washington, DC: Gallaudet University Press.

Sacks, O. 1989. *Seeing Voices: A Journey into the World of the Deaf*. Berkeley, CA: University of California Press.

Winefield, R. 1987. *Never the Twain Shall Meet: Bell, Gallaudet, and the Communications Debate*. Washington, DC: Gallaudet University Press.

Pathological Perspectives of Deafness

> There is no psychology of the deaf. It is, in fact, not clear that there can be one. The term may inevitably represent the pathologizing of cultural differences, the interpretation of difference as deviance. Of course, there are interesting things to be learned and reported about deaf culture, deaf language, and deaf people; the same can be said about many minorities. This knowledge may be found in the literature of that minority, or in works of anthropology, sociology, and sociolinguistics focused on that group. These descriptions are not, however, a "psychology" of the minority and are not offered as such. (H. Lane, 1992: 65)
>
> When the chimpanzee arrived in New York, they named him, whimsically, Nim Chimpsky, after the famous linguist [Noam Chomsky]. ... Laura Petitto had joined the project early, as a volunteer, and had become one of Nim's teachers. It wasn't until Petitto took over that the research was really under control. ... "I was reading the linguistics of ASL, and going down to the Deafness Center. [t]he conversations I has having with deaf signers had nothing in common with what was happening with Nim." ... "There were so many things. Nim's combinations weren't sentences, just strung-out repetitions. There was no syntax, no real exchange of information going on... It wasn't just one thing, there were many, many ways that it wasn't human language." (A. Neisser, 1983: 219-227)

This Unit reviews the medical perspective of deafness: from the physiology of the ear to the signing experiments with non-human primates. While the deaf experience includes the reality that part of the anatomy does not function, the image of being a broken human being does not sit well with the Deaf community. Keep in mind as you read that these issues are not at the forefront of the Deaf community's consciousness and that people who hold only these views of deafness are seen as being paternalistic, prejudiced, and outside of the goals, traditions, and beliefs of the Deaf community.

Section 2 explores the anatomy relevant to Deaf people as visual people who use a manual language for daily communication. You will explore how the eyes, hands and arms work, some causes for disability and how to reduce the damage that can be caused through overuse syndrome.

Look for the answers to the following questions as you read:

1)   What are the significant differences between medical and cultural perspectives of deafness?

2)   What are the components of human anatomy related to hearing?

3)   What are the three main categories of deafness?

4)   How might different causes or ages of onset of deafness affect communication preferences?

5)   How is hearing ability assessed and measured?

6)   What medical interventions exist to treat different forms of deafness?

7)   What is the deaf community's perspective upon these treatments?

8)   What has animal research shown about the nature of language?

9)   What assumptions have been made about signed languages regarding animal research?

10)   What are the components of human anatomy related to sight?

11)   What are some causes of vision loss and blindness?

12)   What are the components of human anatomy related to manual languages?

13)   What are some causes for loss of upper body mobility?

14)   What causes Overuse Syndrome?

15)   How can Overuse Syndrome be prevented or diminished?

Section 1 – Pathological Perspectives of Deafness
Medical and Cultural Perspectives of Deafness

Two contrasting views of deafness direct a significant amount of behavior both within and outside of the deaf community. The Medical View of deafness focuses on the defects of the ear and its resulting effect upon speech clarity and acquisition of the spoken language. The Cultural View of deafness focuses on the abilities of the person and on visual language forms.

Medical Perspectives of deafness are found in a variety of activities and organizations. Alexander Graham Bell's Volta Bureau and organizations which focus on speech training and speech-reading skills work to overcome the disability of deafness. These activities require the deaf person to adjust to the needs of the hearing majority. Mainstreamed school environments often place deaf children in isolation and therefore emphasize their differences from their peers. Audiologists and speech therapists earn their living within the medical perspective of deafness. Hearing aids, while very useful for most people who use them, are part of the medical perspective of deafness. Teachers of deaf children have often been able to blame a child's unwillingness to wear hearing aids for other problems such as poor attention skills and low test scores. Labels such as "hearing-impaired" carry the medical perspective as well because the focus is upon something being broken or damaged.

Cultural Perspectives of deafness are found in many places as well. The National Association of the Deaf, the National Theatre of the Deaf, the American Athletic Association of the Deaf, and many other organizations focus on what deaf people can do or enjoy doing. Residential schools for deaf children allow deaf children to excel or fail in sports or other activities based on their abilities rather than their ability to "overcome" deafness. Storytellers and successful deaf adults provide role models for deaf children to admire. Caption decoding chips in televisions, TTYs, and flashing light signals emphasize what deaf people do well - comprehend the world through their eyes. The label "Deaf" describes what the person is rather than what is missing.

These two perspectives are in marked contrast with one another. Deaf people encounter both every day. Some deaf people will focus on the medical perspective and "internalize" the oppression that it brings. They will see themselves as incomplete or broken, perhaps less than fully human. Other deaf people will focus on the things they can do and spend little time wishing to be something that they are not. The cultural perspective is the more empowering and healthy of the two. A person with the medical perspective of deafness who interacts with deaf people will generally face miscommunication and mutual distrust. A person with the cultural perspective of deafness who interacts with deaf people will generally have good communication and mutual respect.

Washoe and Other Signing Primates

Back in the 1960's there was a movement in psychology known as behaviorism. The basic idea was that we all learn by observation, imitation, and being rewarded for our actions. Actions that are rewarded are reinforced while actions that are not rewarded will not be reinforced. In this way, the theory goes, we all learn to do everything simply because we see other people doing things, such as talking. We try to do those things, and when we make a noise, Mommy smiles. When we make a word, Daddy smiles. As we learn more words and put them into sentences we continue to receive subtle rewards for our achievements.

Two behavioral psychologists, Allen & Beatrice Gardner, decided to take the behavioral view to the extreme. They wanted to test the behavioral view on a chimpanzee. The goal was to see if a chimp could learn to use language. Their argument for why chimps had never learned spoken languages was that the speech anatomy of chimps was different than that of humans. Chimps had never learned to talk because it was physically impossible. But since chimps had full manual capabilities, they argued, chimps might be able to learn a signed language.

The Gardner's established a rich learning environment for their experiment in Reno, Nevada. Washoe, a female chimp, was housed in a trailer with human care givers who surrounded her with signed input for all her waking hours. Finally, after more than a year of this exposure, Washoe produced her first "sign." Actually it was a begging gesture common among apes and chimpanzees, but the Gardner's listed it as the first sign that Washoe used and labeled it "Come/Gimme." As time passed and Washoe was rewarded for attempting to make signs when she saw certain objects, the Gardner's interpreted everything as positive evidence that Washoe was acquiring language.

While we can manipulate and creatively arrange our linguistic symbols, Washoe never learned to actively use her labels linguistically. She could eventually create signs without first seeing the stimulus for them but this was more of a tool-like use of words in order to get food, much like the tool experiments where an ape will grab a stick outside of its cage in order to knock down a bunch of bananas which are suspended from the ceiling.

After five years Washoe had learned less than 150 signs, which comes to an average of about 30 signs a year. The average 2-year-old human knows about 200 words. Other people tried to replicate the Gardners' work but they had conducted their research in secret, releasing only the data that favored their position. One of these replication studies was in New York City with a Chimpanzee named Nim Chimsky (in dubious honor of the linguist, Noam Chomsky). Another was with a gorilla named Koko. Nim learned 125 signs by the age of 4. Koko seemed to progress the most - attaining a productive vocabulary of about 400 signs. Other researchers quickly came to the conclusion that there were no inherent language capabilities in Washoe or any other chimpanzee. All of these accomplishments could be explained as animal training. The key factor missing from all of the animal communication was syntax. The animals could communicate, but no rules governed their communication, therefore they did not have language.

Human use of language is marked by incredible productivity. We can create brand new sentences and we do so all the time. This creates a problem for behaviorists because we are able to create sentences we have never heard or seen before. Therefore we are not imitating or copying things that we observe but are actively inventing. The researchers observed these primates' *symbolic* and *interactive* communication. The erroneously believed it was actually language - none of these primates have ever demonstrated any *rule-governed productive ability*, nor have any taught these signs to a *second generation*. The research clearly shows that animals can easily *communicate*, but **language** is **uniquely a human capability**.

Components of the Ear

With the respect that physicians have as experts it can be hard to convince a person within the medical perspective of deafness that the cultural perspective has significant value; and yet professionals working with the Deaf community will often find themselves needing to communicate with or between people holding this perspective. It may be necessary to establish communication first by demonstrating one's knowledge about the ear before attempting to educate a person about the cultural perspective of the Deaf community. This Unit explores the medical perspective beginning with the anatomy of the ear.

The ear is divided into three parts: the Outer Ear, Middle Ear, and Inner Ear. These components provide a link between the sound waves in the environment and the perception of sound by the human brain. The outer ear depends on air to conduct sound information to the eardrum. The middle ear depends on mechanical motion to conduct sound information to the oval window. The inner ear depends on movement of fluid to conduct sound information to the hair cells in the cochlea where the information is converted to electrical stimulus, which the auditory nerve then conducts to the auditory cortex of the brain.

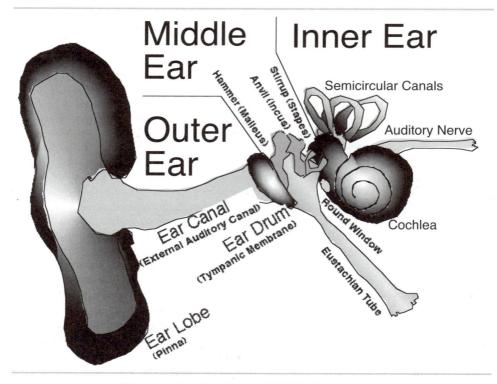

Figure 3.1 – The Outer, Middle & Inner Ear

The Outer Ear – Air Conduction

The Outer Ear consists of the ear lobe (*pinna*), the ear canal (*external auditory canal*), and the eardrum (*tympanic membrane*). These components are all visible and somewhat exposed to the environment. The ear lobe focuses sound into the ear canal. Every person's ear lobes are unique, even to the extent that the left and right ear lobes are not mirror images of each other. The ear canal is filled with hair cells and wax, which help prevent contaminants from reaching the eardrum. The eardrum is a thin cover of skin, which seals off the middle ear from the outside environment. The eardrum vibrates as sound waves come into contact with it.

The Middle Ear – Mechanical Conduction

The Middle Ear consists of three bones, which connect the eardrum to the inner ear. These bones magnify the vibrations of the eardrum. The first bone (*malleus*) is commonly called the "hammer", the second (*incus*) is called the "anvil", and the third (*stapes*) is called the stirrups. If these bones are fused together they will result in what is known as a "conductive" hearing loss, meaning that the bones cannot move effectively and therefore the sound waves are not being properly conducted to the inner ear. Conductive losses can be corrected surgically, usually by replacing the fused bones.

The Inner Ear – Fluid Conduction

The Inner Ear consists of the Cochlea, the Oval window, and the Semicircular canals. The third bone of the middle ear (the stapes) rests directly upon the Oval Window. The Oval Window is flexible and allows the movement of the last bone of the middle ear (the stapes) to be transferred to movement of the liquid inside the inner ear. Another flexible portion of the cochlea, the Round Window, allows for the equalization of pressure caused by the movement of fluid in the cochlea. The cochlea is filled with fluid and the movement of this fluid causes hair cells inside the cochlea to vibrate. These vibrations are converted to electrical information and conveyed by the auditory nerve (the eighth cranial nerve) to the auditory cortex where the brain perceives this information as sound. If the hair cells are damaged or if the cochlea contains no fluid, the result is known as a "sensory-neural" hearing loss. This kind of hearing loss cannot currently be corrected through surgery, although there is an implant that can bypass this type of damage to a very limited extent.

Also part of the Inner Ear, the Semicircular Canals provide the sense of balance. They contain fluid that moves when the head shifts positions. Damage to this part of the inner ear can cause problems with balance and often co-occurs with hearing loss.

Together these components provide a very intricate and sensitive means of accessing sound information. It is rather amazing that all these components work together for the majority of people and that deafness is not a more common phenomenon. Because of these intricacies, there are limited ways of correcting hearing loss. Hearing aids only amplify sounds, which still must travel through the rest of the existing structures mentioned above. Implantation surgery bypasses all of the outer and middle ear components as well as some portions of the inner ear, but because of the small size of the cochlea, this solution only provides limited access to sounds as they are processed and conveyed through no more than twenty-three distinct channels of information.

Causes of Deafness

The causes of deafness can be divided into three main categories: 1) genetic deafness, 2) deafness caused by illness or trauma, and 3) loss of hearing with age. Genetic causes of deafness are caused by strong genes that carry the trait of deafness being passed from one generation to another. Some genetic causes of deafness will be passed to each generation as long as one parent carries the gene. Other genetic causes of deafness require *both* the mother and father to pass the genetic trait to their offspring. Genetic causes of deafness constitute a minority of the cases of deafness.

One genetic cause of deafness also includes a progressive reduction of vision. This is called Usher Syndrome and has a variety of specific types associated with it. Generally they include early onset of deafness (some versions have a progressive loss) and around puberty retinitis pigmentosa becomes obvious as peripheral vision is slowly diminished. Most people with Usher syndrome will be fully DeafBlind in their thirties.

Illness and trauma may cause deafness prior to birth or after birth. This distinction is known as *congenital* (prior to birth) and *adventitious* (after birth). A further distinction is made for adventitious deafness: prelingual and postlingual, meaning that the onset of deafness was before or after two years of age when a child is normally demonstrating control of two-word utterances. **Postlingual** deafness means that the child has made significant progress on a first language prior to becoming deaf and may still be able to function as a native user even if it is a spoken language. **Prelingual** deafness means that the child is likely to have more difficulty making a spoken language their first and native language and that a predictably better choice would be to develop a signed language as their first language (or at least choose a completely visual representation of a spoken language).

The primary illnesses that cause deafness are generally related to high fever. Leading causes include spinal meningitis and scarlet fever. The high fever damages the hair cells in the cochlea, therefore reducing their ability to transmit sound information to the auditory nerve. German measles, otherwise known as Rubella, also can cause deafness to unborn children if their mother contracts the disease during her pregnancy. A large number of deaf children were born in the 1960s and are often referred to as the "Rubella bulge".

Head trauma is the most likely cause of traumatic deafness. Automobile accidents are a common cause of this kind of deafness. Some people have become deaf as part of an allergic reaction to medication. Exposure to loud bursts of noise such as explosions or to sustained loud volumes such as electric guitars and drums can also lead to hearing loss. People who experience traumatic deafness are generally older, perhaps even finished with their basic education and living lives with no understanding or anticipation of any need to know about deafness. These people often experience significant psychological side effects from a sudden loss of hearing. They may experience a prolonged period of denial and hold out hope for restoration of their hearing for years or even decades. Late-deafened adults generally retain their ability to speak but become frustrated by being unable to understand responses from other people. They may strongly resist using signed languages as an obvious admission that they are no longer able to hear, resulting in greater isolation from both hearing and deaf people.

As adults become older many experience a gradual loss of hearing. Senior citizens may be unaware of their gradual loss of hearing. Initially they may benefit from auditory amplification such as through hearing aids but if the loss progresses they may function more like the late deafened adults mentioned above.

Audiograms and Decibels

One of the most common scientific ways of measuring hearing loss is to measure the volume levels required to perceive various kinds of sound. Upon suspicion that a child is deaf, the child is likely to receive specialized testing designed to provide specific information about the nature of the child's deafness. To understand the results of this testing, called an audiogram, we must first understand a little bit about the nature of sound.

Sound has a variety of frequencies from very low-pitched sounds to very high pitched sounds. **Frequency** is measured in *Hertz*, which is named in honor of Heinrich Rudolf Hertz, a German physicist. One Hertz (Hz) is equal to one full cycle (of sound variation) in one second. Humans are unable to detect sounds of very low frequencies or of very high frequencies. Generally people can hear sounds as low as 80 Hz and as high as 8,000 Hz. Our skin is also sensitive to sound but in very limited ways. We cannot "hear" with our skin, but we can feel the presence of low-pitched sounds in the 200 - 800 Hz range.

Independent of the frequency is the level of volume or loudness. **Volume** is measured in *Decibels* (dB) which are named in honor of Alexander Graham Bell. The higher the number of decibels, the louder the volume of the sound. Audiograms record these two variables (frequency and volume) within the range of human hearing.

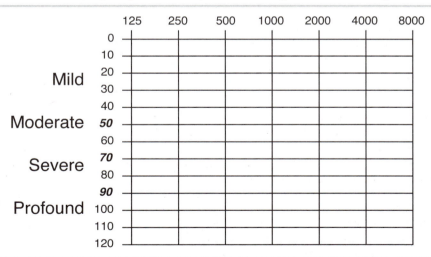

Figure 3.2 – Audiogram Variables (Decibels & Frequencies)

One other variable of sound production not measured in audiograms is sound **duration** (simply measured in seconds or fractions of seconds). This is relevant to using an audiogram to predict speech perception because the duration of sounds in speech tends to be very short. Audiological testing may more realistically reflect the duration of warning signals (car horns, alarms, etc.) rather than speech sounds. The audiogram simply records the threshold, or point where a particular sound can be perceived. Generally an audiogram will be attained using "pure tones." Pure tones are isolated sounds of only one frequency. Speech is not produced in pure tones, but rather mixes many frequencies all at the same time. The audiogram does not provide details of the quality of sound or of the usefulness of sound toward perceiving and controlling one's own speech.

Cochlear Implants

The ear has three primary parts: the outer ear, the middle ear, and the inner ear. Defects with the outer ear can be corrected surgically if necessary, by reconstruction of the ear lobe, ear canal, or the eardrum. Middle ear defects are more likely to result in loss of sound perception. The middle ear consists of three bones that connect the eardrum (outer ear) to the oval window (inner ear). Previously this kind of hearing loss was not correctable, but it can now be corrected surgically by manipulating or replacing the bones of the middle ear.

The inner ear is the area of the ear that remains beyond the reach of complete correction through medical intervention. The inner ear consists of the semi-circular canals (which provide our sense of balance) and the cochlea. The cochlea is a spiraling tube filled with fluid and lined with tiny hair cells. These hair cells detect movement in the fluid (initiated by the moving bones of the middle ear) and convert this movement into electrical signals that are picked up by auditory nerves below the hair cells. The auditory nerves take these signals and convey them to the brain where they are perceived as sound.

Damage to the inner ear is typically related to the hair cells in the cochlea. A process was developed to bypass this problem with inner ear deafness. Dr. William House and an engineer developed a single electrode designed to convey electrical information to the auditory nerve. This electrode, and its related equipment, could be used to take sound through a microphone, into a processor, and then through wires to the electrode inside the cochlea. This procedure bypasses the outer ear, middle ear, and parts of the inner ear to electronically stimulate an auditory nerve.

This surgery was performed successfully for several patients and these patients were able to "hear" a single signal that represented a very narrow range of sounds. If there was a sound within that range then the implanted person would know that there was a sound, but had little additional information to define or use the sound. An additional concern was that these initial surgeries left an open socket in the head that left the implanted person with a life-time risk for infection.

The solutions to these problems would include 1) the use of a signal transmitter and a receiver to allow the implant to receive information without installing a connection port on the scalp and 2) the ability to connect to more auditory nerves and convey broader ranges of sound to the brain. An Australian company set out to develop just such solutions and came up with a 22-electrode device, which is still being used in cochlear implantation surgeries world-wide. The general procedure is the same as the single-electrode device but the processing of the sound and how the signals are delivered to the brain is enhanced. Sound is still detected through a microphone, processed, but is sent through wires to a small transmitter which is held magnetically over the location of the implant a few inches behind the ear. The implanted portion now has a receiver that picks up the processed information and sends it through a series of electrodes, which are evenly spaced apart so that inside the cochlea each individual electrode is in contact with different auditory nerves. One of the electrodes served as a conductor, leaving only 21 electrodes to convey distinct sets of electrical information to the auditory nerve, which then transmits this information to the brain where it is perceived as sound (see diagram, below). A newer model now exists which has 24 electrodes and allows for all 24 electrodes to deliver sound information.

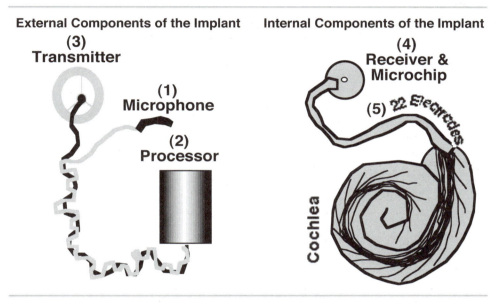

Figure 3.3 - Components of the Cochlear Implant

Each specific range of sound is received by the processor and then delivered through the implant as a single signal to the brain. Because there is variety in the signals reaching the brain, the brain has more information and has a better chance of making sense of the information. But 21 channels of information does not compare to the thousands of distinct frequencies that the ear is naturally capable of. While there are sufficient auditory nerves to convey thousands of distinct signals from the cochlea to the brain; the implant can't even deliver two dozen distinct signals.

People who have heard before and lost their hearing seem to benefit most from cochlear implants. They already have an understanding of sound, which helps them make sense of the signals processed through the implant. People who have been deaf from birth can also benefit but the results are very unpredictable. Some are able to use the implant to monitor their own speech production to the point that other people can understand most of what they say. Others seem to get minimal benefits from the implant surgery. Some people have eventually chosen not to use the implant at all.

There may be measurable advantages to receiving sound through a cochlear implant rather than through a severely damaged cochlea, but the implant is far from adequate in comparison with natural hearing. Efforts are underway to pursue cochlear transplants, which may be the only way to ever provide natural sound to the brain of a person with inner-ear deafness. The challenge with transplants would be making the connections of hundreds or thousands of auditory nerves to the new cochlea.

Several significant dangers surround the surgery. First is that the procedure takes place between two sets of nerves. If these nerves are damaged then the patient's sense of smell or ability to move one side of their face will be irreversibly damaged. The second danger is that when the wires and electrodes are placed into the inner ear, they pass through the round window, which releases some of the fluid of the inner ear. This fluid is required for our sense of balance, therefore Cochlear Implant recipients may receive permanent damage to their internal ability to maintain balance.

The Deaf Community's Perspective of Cochlear Implants

Section 1 of this Unit has provided an overview of the major elements of deafness from the medical perspective. This perspective views the deaf person as an impaired, incomplete person. This perspective of deafness is often connected with money in that experts hired to fix deafness often receive high salaries (doctors, speech pathologists, audiologists). The medical perspective focuses on the inability of the deaf person; any success in hearing, or in generating clear speech, cannot be directly monitored by the deaf person - meaning that they are dependant upon others for feedback toward success. Likewise their self-esteem is heavily impacted by skills over which they have little control. Many members of the Deaf community will view hearing aids and the use of speech as symbols of disempowerment and dependency.

The cultural perspective of Deafness regards Deaf people as sharing a trait, which leads them to a shared culture and language. The use of visual communication is highly valued along with the freedom to use signed languages. While historically signing was prohibited and taught as being an indication of low intelligence or low social status, now some Deaf people will make it a point of personal pride to communicate visually even if they do have usable speech-reading and speaking skills. Many Deaf people with intelligible speech choose not to use their voice with strangers who often misunderstand imperfect speech to be associated with mental retardation or with inebriation. An empowered Deaf person will seek to live in a way that they focus on the abilities that they have rather than on a disability.

When cochlear implants first became available to the public the Deaf community almost unanimously was against the procedure. Costing thousands of dollars and hundreds of hours of speech therapy in order to be effective, implantation was seen as yet another money making scam for the medical profession at the financial, physical, and emotional expense of the Deaf community. Many people who pursued the single-channel implants found them relatively useless (although others still make use of such implants decades after the surgery).

As the technology improved the allowable age for implant surgeries was reduced. Initially a deaf child had to be over the age of two to be a candidate for the surgery. This was rather alarming for members of the Deaf community: adults can make informed decisions about this surgery but children having surgery which would impact their self identity seemed only possible in science fiction or totalitarian regimes. Surgery is now allowed for infants only a few months old.

There are sound medical and developmental reasons for having the surgery by the age of 6 months: this reduces the amount of effort needed by the child to make effective use of the device since the brain is most pliable in the first two years of life.

From a cultural perspective, however, implantation is an act of genocide because the Deaf community depends largely on the deaf children of hearing parents (90 % of the Deaf community) in order to exist. If the deaf child is able to make effective use of a cochlear implant then that child no longer has an obvious need for signed language. Since cochlear implants still do not come close to providing normal hearing the implanted child may still actually have a biological need for signed language, but would be much more resistant to recognizing that need since they would not likely associate with other Deaf children.

The National Association of the Deaf initially took an oppositional stand against implant surgery. In the year 2000 the NAD formally recognized that deaf adults with cochlear implants can still serve a vital role in the goals of the NAD and therefore the NAD moved to a neutral stand on implant surgery.

Section 2 – Anatomy of Visual/Manual Communication
Components of the Eye

Deaf people widely regard themselves as "visual" people. Signed languages are naturally suited to visual perception, not depending upon sound in their production or perception. The eye is a complex mechanism that allows the brain to perceive images.

The eye is a hollow sphere divided into three layers (called *tunics*). The outer *Fibrous Tunic* is composed of the cornea in the front and the sclera surrounding the remainder of the eye. The *cornea* is the clear portion, which allows light to enter into the eye. The *sclera* is composed of tougher connective tissue, which keeps the shape of the eye and also provides a way for muscles to attach to the eye.

The middle *Vascular Tunic* has three subdivisions: the Iris, the Ciliary Body, and the Choroid. The *iris* is the pigmented circular material that is positioned directly behind the cornea. The iris expands (constricting the pupil) to reduce the amount of light entering the eye and it diminishes (dilating the pupil) to allow more light to enter. The *ciliary body* itself has several components. The *ciliary processes* generate the fluid, which fills the eye. This fluid is called the *aqueous humor*. *Ciliary muscles* are attached to the lens with *suspensory ligaments* and allow the lens to be pulled into different shapes to focus light within the eye. The *choroid* is the remaining 5/6 of the vascular tunic and provides a dark brown, non-reflective surface which absorbs excess light in the eye.

The inner *Nervous Tunic* is also known as the *retina* and has two kinds of photoreceptor cells: cones and rods. *Cones* respond to three different colors (red, green and blue) of bright light and are concentrated at the center of the rear portion of the retina. This area of the retina is called the *macula lutea* and corresponds to what we perceive as the center of our vision. *Rods* respond to dim light and provide greater perception of motion, but less perception of color.

The lens provides a division between the front of the eye. The anterior cavity is in front of the lens and is filled with a clear liquid called the aqueous humor. This fluid is replenished and provides both oxygen and pressure to the components of the anterior cavity. The posterior cavity is behind the lens and is filled with a clear liquid called the vitreous humor. This fluid is in place from birth and is not replenished.

Vision occurs when light passes through the lens, which refracts the light that hits the retina. Cones and rods in the retina generate a neurotransmitter which create nerve impulses that travel along the two optic nerves. Half of each eye's vision field is processed by the same hemisphere of the brain. In other words, the left half of each eye is processed in the left hemisphere while the right half of each eye is processed in the right hemisphere.

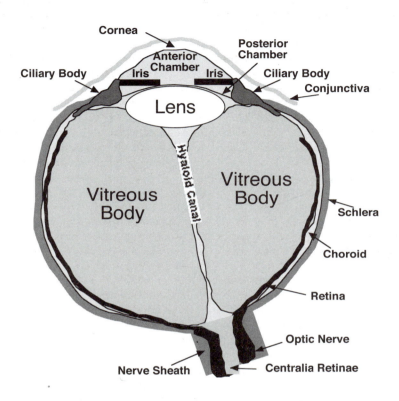

Figure 3.4 - The Anatomy of the Eye

Causes of Vision Loss and Blindness

The causes of vision loss and blindness can be divided into four main categories: 1) genetic blindness, 2) blindness caused by illness 3) blindness caused by trauma, and 4) loss of vision with age. Genetic causes of blindness are caused by strong genes that carry the trait of blindness being passed from one generation to another. One genetic cause of blindness is *retinitis pigmentosa* which is a degeneration of the retina and the choroid. The condition begins to have its effects between the ages of ten and twelve years. The initial effects are an increasing restriction of peripheral vision (often referred to as "tunnel vision) and night blindness where the rods are less and less effective in detecting lower light levels.

The condition called Usher Syndrome combines deafness (or a progressive hearing loss) with Retinitis Pigmentosa. Generally there is an early onset of deafness (some versions have a progressive loss) and around puberty retinitis pigmentosa becomes obvious as peripheral vision is slowly diminished. Most people with Usher syndrome will be fully DeafBlind in their thirties. There are no cures for these genetic conditions.

Illness and trauma may cause blindness prior to birth or after birth. The specific causes of vision loss can vary but include cataracts, glaucoma, and macular degeneration. *Cataracts* are a clouding of the lens and can be corrected with surgery. *Glaucoma* is caused by increasing pressure in the anterior cavity when the aqueous humor builds up rather than draining properly. Medication and/or surgery can provide correction, especially in earlier stages. *Macular degeneration* is a breakdown of the central-vision portion of the retina, the macula. Laser treatments can provide some benefit. One interesting side effect of this condition is that peripheral vision is generally still effective and thus people with the condition are forced to look slightly away from objects to see them. This effect can cause consternation from communication partners who may believe that a person with macular degeneration is distracted or not paying attention. Macular degeneration is a kind of opposite of the "tunnel vision" of retinitis pigmentosa which means that a person with both conditions will have their vision reduced to an irregular ring and may need to "sweep" their eyes from side to side to see effectively.

One additional condition – diabetic retinopathy – is tied to diabetes and occurs when blood vessels in the eye change, sometimes bursting and clouding the vitreous humor, or causing a detachment of the retina from the back of the eye. Laser surgeries can provide significant improvement if done early.

Eye Examinations and Correction

One of the most common scientific ways of measuring visual acuity is to determine the sharpness of vision at a distance of twenty feet. The term 20/20 vision indicates that a person can see something twenty feet away with the clarity that they should see from twenty feet. This does not mean that a person can read fine print from twenty feet distance. An assessment of 20/40 means that the visual acuity that a person should have at 40 feet is only achieved at twenty feet of distance. This level (20/40) is a standard requirement for qualifying for a drivers license in many states. Visual acuity rated at 20/200 or worse is considered legal blindness.

Although anyone can be trained to provide a visual acuity assessment, causes of reduced acuity should be identified by doctors of optometry. An optometrist can prescribe glasses and/or contact lenses. If optometrists detect an eye disease, they may prescribe medication or treatment by an ophthalmologist.

Components of the Arms and Hands

The entire human body contains 206 bones. 80 of these are on the midline (center) of the body and include the 22 bones of the face and skull, and the 6 bones of the middle ear (in two sets of three bones per ear). The remaining 126 bones are located to either side of the midline and are divided equally between the upper and lower body: 60 in the upper limbs (arms and hands) and 60 in the lower limbs (legs and feet). Two bones connect the legs to the midline (hip bones). Four bones connect the arms to the midline (collarbones and shoulder blades).

American Sign language makes significant use of the 60 bones in the upper body limbs. Each arm has a single bone in the upper arm (the *humerus*), two bones in the forearm (*ulna* and *radius*), eight bones in the wrist (the *carpals*), five bones in the palm (*metacarpals*) and fourteen bones in the fingers and thumb (*phalanges*). The arms are suspended from the collarbone (*clavicle*) and the shoulder blade (*scapula*).

Joints occur at the point where two (or more) bones meet. All of the bones of the arm are *synovial joints*, which have a fluid-filled cavity between the bones of the joint. Synovial joints are also known as *diarthrosis* joints, which mean that they are designed to be freely moveable. ASL makes significant use of the free mobility of the arm, hand, and fingers. This free mobility allows a very broad variety of contrasting configurations and placements within signing space. ASL does not make use of all possible configurations; the configurations that are used do not occur at the extreme or painful ranges of potential motion.

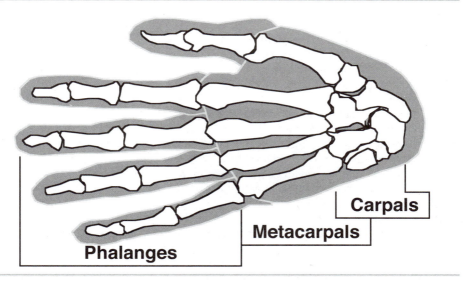

Figure 3.5- The Bones of the Hand

Finger and Thumb Dexterity

Each hand (including the wrist) is composed of twenty-seven bones. The thumb is positioned so that it can freely rotate and move to oppose the palm and fingers. This allows the pad of the thumb to contact each of the twelve finger joints and the four fingertips (sixteen distinct contact points). The extended fingers can move in two directions, forward/backward and side-to-side. This allows fourteen different configurations of forward/backward movement at the base joint (independent of thumb posture) and eight different configurations of side-to-side groupings. Each of the four fingers can also bend at the two remaining joints, though generally the distal joint does not bend significantly without the medial joint also bending. This provides three additional contrasting configurations for each finger.

Multiplying these thumb and finger configurations provides a minimum of 5,376 unique potential hand postures. This entire set could then be doubled by having the thumb positioned proximally (but not actually contacting) the sixteen distinct contact points mentioned above. So it is at least theoretically possible to generate over 10,000 technically distinct handshapes; but many of these handshapes are not *visually* distinct.

Thumb contact with the tip of the fingers can be visually confused with contacting the distal joint. Contact with the base joint can be visually confused with contacting the medial joint. Bending of the medial joint alone can be visually confused with bending of both the medial and distal joints. Even with these reductions there are still 3,584 possible *visually* distinct handshapes.

From this set, some are more *physically comfortable* to produce than others. The ring and middle fingers move more comfortably together than in isolation. Thumb contacts with the base joints of the fingers are generally more difficult than contact with the fingertips. These adjustments reduce the possible number to 896 handshapes that are BOTH reasonably comfortable AND visually distinct.

ASL appears to use only about one sixth of these approximately 900 potential handshapes: Liddell and Johnson (1989) determined more than 150 hand configurations in ASL lexical signs. Earlier estimates of the number of handshapes in ASL were lower than 60 (Stokoe, 1960; Klima, 1975; Newkirk, 1975; Battison, 1978).

Wrist Movement

Independent of handshape is wrist configuration. The wrist is composed of eight bones, which are designed to glide and twist to allow forward/backward movement, side-to-side movement, and (in conjunction with forearm movement) rotation. Rotation of the palm so that the finger pads would be able to touch the shoulder is called *pronation*. The reverse rotation is called *supination*. Forward movement is called *flexion*, backward movement is *hyperextension* (straight out is called *extension*). Movement tilting toward the thumb side *is radial flexion*, tilting to the opposite side *is ulnar flexion*. These last two movements are not widely used in ASL.

Arm Extension

ASL makes many signs in what is known as "neutral space" which places the hands in front of the body, above the waist, below the chin, and between the shoulders. This three-dimensional space can be *proximal* (close to the body), *medial* (in between), or *distal* (far from the body). These distances from the body are achieved through bending the arm at the elbow and/or extending the arm from shoulder. Distal locations in neutral space have minimal bending of the elbow while more proximal locations have greater amounts of bending at the elbow, generally close to a right angle for medial space and acute angles for proximal space.

Loss of Mobility in the Hands and Arms

The causes of reduced or restricted mobility of fingers, thumb, wrist, elbow, and/or shoulder joints can be divided into four main categories: 1) congenital limitations, 2) damage caused by illness 3) damage caused by trauma, and 4) loss of mobility with age.

Genetic causes include cerebral palsy, which diminishes the communication between the brain and the body's muscles. The result of this miscommunication is reduced control of muscles and can vary from minor loss of fine motor skills to significant loss of gross motor skills. Cerebral palsy can be caused by lack of oxygen to the brain. Human communication can be impacted because spoken language, written language, and signed language all require muscle movements. There is no cure for cerebral palsy, but it is possible to build and train muscle response to improve enough to be functional/useful. It is also possible to provide substitution communication techniques, which take advantage of the most controllable muscles, such as eye movement or head movement, for example.

Similar communication restrictions can occur through Multiple Sclerosis, Parkinson's disease, and Lou Gehrig's disease. These conditions can involve diminished muscle strength and/or can involve delays or miscommunication between the brain and the muscles in ways somewhat similar to cerebral palsy.

> **Amyotrophic Lateral Sclerosis (Lou Gehrig's disease)** - thickening of tissue in the motor tracts of the lateral columns and anterior horns of the spinal cord; results in progressive muscle atrophy that starts in the limbs.[11]

> **Muscular dystrophy** - Muscular dystrophy refers to any one of a group of muscle diseases in which there is a recognizable pattern of inheritance. They are marked by weakness and wasting of selected muscles. The affected muscle fibers degenerate and are replaced by fatty tissue. The dystrophies are classified according to the patient's age at onset, distribution of the weakness, progression of the disease, and mode of inheritance. The most common form is Duchenne dystrophy, which is inherited as a sex-linked recessive gene and is nearly always restricted to boys. It usually begins before the age of four, with weakness and wasting of the muscles of the pelvis and back.

> **Parkinson's disease (parkinsonism)** - a chronic progressive nerve disease characterized by muscle tremors, weakness, rigid movements, halting gait, drooping posture and expressionless facial appearance.

One genetic cause of deafness also includes a progressive reduction of vision. This is called Usher Syndrome, which has a variety of specific types associated with it. Generally they include early onset of deafness (some versions have a progressive loss) and around puberty retinitis pigmentosa becomes obvious as peripheral vision is slowly diminished. Most people with Usher syndrome will be fully DeafBlind in their thirties.

Illness and trauma may cause reduction of mobility. Arthritis is one such condition, which is an inflammation of the joints. Broken bones and the ligaments that connect the bones at joints can also fail to heal correctly, causing physical discomfort. Various conditions include *tendonitis* (inflammation of the tendons that connect bone to muscle) to carpal tunnel syndrome or *tenosynovitis* (inflammation of the protective sheath surrounding the tendon).

---

[11] These three definitions are from "Google web definitions" citing neurolab.jsc.nasa.gov/glossim.htm

Overuse Syndrome and Stress Management

Overuse syndrome is a potential hazard in any profession that requires repeated muscular movement. Assembly line workers, athletes, musicians, keyboard operators, and interpreters are all susceptible to injury through the repetitious movement of arm, hand, finger, leg, back, and neck muscles. The injuries that signed language interpreters face are most commonly related to the wrist, although fingers, upper arms, shoulders, and the neck may be involved as well.

There are many myths about overuse syndrome and sign language interpreters. Some people believe that native signers do not suffer from O.S. But there are indeed many native signers working as interpreters who do get O.S. Some people think that deaf people are immune or people who are both deaf and native signers are immune. The facts do not support these myths. Anyone can be susceptible to Overuse Syndrome simply by doing what its name says: over-use.

The symptoms of Overuse Syndrome are simple enough: numbness and/or pain. The levels of pain are progressive: pain when the muscles are in use, pain in between uses, pain for several hours after use, constant and unending pain, pain that is so severe that it disturbs sleep. The point at which you should become aware and begin to take action is the very first one. If your muscles hurt just doing your job, then the way you do your job is probably causing the pain and needs to be reviewed. Do you put pressure on the base of your wrists? This might happen for keyboard operators who rest the weight of their hands on the base of their wrists while typing. While the fingers are typing, muscles and tendons are moving throughout the hand and wrists. With pressure being applied to the base of the wrists, this finger movement causes unnecessary friction, wear, and tear. The solution may be to reduce the pressure (support the hands in a different way) and also, perhaps, to reduce the amount of time spent doing data entry.

Overuse Syndrome can come from cumulative trauma. Do you drive with your hands flexed back (thus increasing the pressure at the wrist)? Do you sleep with you head applying pressure to any part of your hands? Do you do keyboard work in addition to interpreting? Do you drive a stick shift car? Do you use a hand-held basket when shopping rather than a cart with wheels? Do you carry a heavy bag or purse for long periods of time? Do you lift children or heavy packages frequently? Do you shake your hand rapidly when you use a hairdryer? Do you use your hands or arms to support your head during classroom lectures? It is entirely possible that the act of using sign language by itself is not traumatic to your hands, wrist, arms, shoulders, or neck. The trauma may occur due to the cumulative effect of several factors.

The most obvious solution is to stop hurting yourself and to stop now. But in order to stop you have to catch yourself doing things that put you at risk. Think about what you are doing with your hands when you are not signing. How do you support your weight with your arms and hands? Do you have any sensations of short and sharp pain, or even dull and prolonged pain? Determine what might cause the pain... can you change that behavior?

Another entire area of concern is emotional stress. When we are experiencing emotional stress, we tend to physically tense our muscles. The solution is the same: identify what causes emotional stress. Do you find yourself clenching your teeth in certain situations? Determine what is causing you to become tense: the people you are with, the setting, the topic, your comfort with your ability to do your job... all of these are potential stress-causing factors. Another common reaction to stress, particularly among

ASL and Interpreting students, is raising the shoulders while signing. This can cause neck and shoulder tension leading to general pain or tension headaches. This tightened posture also results in the appearance of being overly emphatic in ASL production.

Next you should determine what things help to ease stress. Dancing, physical exercise, and listening to fast-paced music may relieve stress. Swimming, meditation, massage, or listening to slow, instrumental music may relieve stress. Become aware of the personal activities that help you to feel better about yourself and make the time to enjoy these activities.

With attention to the way you do your work and they way you do your relaxation it is possible to prevent Overuse Syndrome and at the same time to enjoy your work. While some surgeries can reduce pain or provide some amount of comfort, there are few solutions as effective as prevention.

Summary

     This Unit presented a variety of aspects of pathological, or medical, perspectives of deafness. These perspectives have often served to subjugate deaf people to the beliefs of medical specialists who often stand to benefit financially by identifying disability or inferiority in others. The physical attributes of deafness do serve as part of membership in the deaf community; and certain linguistic and cultural preferences may be better understood by investigating these areas (such as why deaf people would prefer to use a visual/gestural language to associate with other people inclined to use such a language). The myth of a psychology of the deaf is presented to provide contrast between how deaf people see themselves (an empowered culture of intelligent people) and how the majority culture still views them (a disabled population needing medical and social assistance).

Ear Anatomy

Label each element below. Identify which parts belong to the outer ear, the middle ear, and the inner ear. Which elements are significant for various surgical interventions?

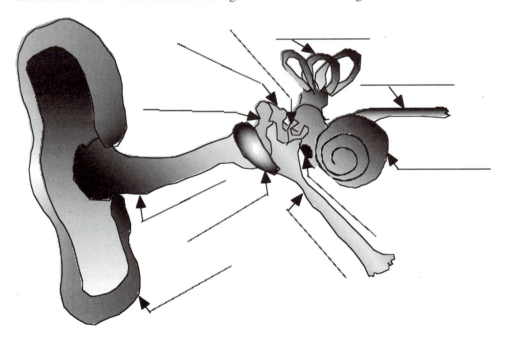

Section 1 Review Questions

1) What are some of the main differences between the medical and cultural perspectives of deafness?

2) What are the main components of the outer ear?

3) What are the main components of the middle ear?

4) What are the main components of the inner ear?

5) What are the three main categories of deafness?

6) What do the following terms mean?

> Congenital Deafness   Adventitious Deafness
>
> Prelingual Deafness   Postlingual Deafness

7) What two variables are measured by audiograms?

8) Why might two people with identical audiograms still have very different abilities to hear?

9) What are the external components of a cochlear implant?

10) Where are the internal components of a cochlear implant placed during surgery?

11) What was the name of the signing primate in Nevada?

12) What was the name of the signing primate in New York City?

13) What aspects of communication did the signing primates achieve?

14) What aspects of language did the signing primates fail to achieve?

Eye Anatomy
Label each element below.

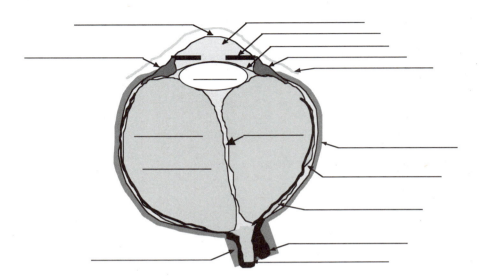

Section 2 Review Questions

15) Identify three components of the eye which light passes through.

16) Identify three causes of vision loss.

17) How many non-midline bones are in the upper limbs?

18) How many bones are in each hand and wrist (combined)?

19) What are the three major labels for the bones of the hand?

20) Which side of the hand is the ulnar side?

21) Identify three causes of mobility loss.

22) What is Overuse Syndrome?

23) Identify five common activities that can lead to overuse syndrome in the hands and arms

24) How can Overuse Syndrome be prevented or treated?

25) Identify three ways to reduce stress.

Human Anatomy and the Ear

Bloom, F. E. & A. Lazerson. 1988. *Brain, Mind, and Behavior: Second Edition.* New York, NY: W. H. Freeman and Company.

Snell, R. S. 1978. *Atlas of Clinical Anatomy.* Boston, MA: Little, Brown, and Company.

Audiology and Cochlear Implantation

Crabtree, M. & J. Powers, Eds. *Language Files: Materials for an Introduction to Language.* Columbus Ohio: Ohio State University Press.

Crystal, D. 1987. *The Cambridge Encyclopedia of Language.* New York, NY: Cambridge University Press.

Lane, H. 1992. The Mask of Benevolence: Disabling the Deaf Community. New York: Alfred A. Knopf.

Primate Language Studies

Neisser, A. 1983. *The Other Side of Silence: Sign Language and the Deaf Community in America.* Washington, DC: Gallaudet University Press.

Valli, C. 1996. Personal Communication.

The Linguistics of American Sign Language and English Within the Deaf Community

It would be difficult to overestimate the effect that Bill Stokoe's work has had on deaf people in this country. That work began soon after he arrived at Gallaudet to teach Chaucer and other English writers and poets, and to work again with his best friend. Here were two humanists: George, a Shakespearian scholar with a passion for theatre; and Bill, an expert on Chaucer and other Old and Middle English authors, who had absolutely no knowledge of or experience with deaf students. Who would ever have guessed that Gallaudet, its deaf faculty and students, and the lives of hundreds of thousands of deaf people would be so changed by their presence there? Although it was Bill Stokoe who first made revolutionary observations and discoveries about American Sign Language, although it was he who publicized them and encouraged other scholars and researchers to develop these observations further and to apply them, it was George Detmold who fought with the administration, with the faculty, even with the students, to enable Bill to have the time, the space, and the funding necessary to proceed. Thirty-five years later, the work of Bill Stokoe, supported by George Detmold, would come to fruition in the form of one of the most dramatic expressions of justice and equality for deaf people ever to occur. When I. King Jordan declared in 1988 that "deaf people can do anything but hear," he was expressing a belief that was new to most people in the United States, but Bill Stokoe and George Detmold had known it all along. (J. Maher, 1993: 14-15)

This Unit reviews the issues of language research and bilingualism within the deaf community, including the interaction of ASL and English within the Deaf community. You will come to understand the contributions made by William Stokoe and the numerous researchers that followed his lead.

Section 2 explores the variety of communication preferences that exist within the Deaf community, including oral communication and the communication needs of DeafBlind people. Various inventions for assisting deaf children in the acquisition of English are also presented.

Look for the answers to the following questions as you read:

1) What contributions did William Stokoe make toward linguistic research of signed languages?

2) What impact did Bill Stokoe's research have upon the deaf community?

3) What label did Bill Stokoe assign to language variation in the deaf community?

4) What label did James Woodward assign to language variation in the deaf community?

5) What kinds of spoken-language / written-language encoding tools are used by deaf people?

6) What other labels have been applied to the use of ASL between deaf and hearing people?

7) What factors limit the ability to co-produce English and ASL?

8) Why would some deaf people want to improve their speech / speechreading skills?

9) What adaptations should be considered for communicating with DeafBlind people?

10) What is the primary purpose of Cueing?

11) What three parameters of signed languages are also present in the production of manual cues?

12) What assumptions were made regarding ASL and its modifications through Manual English Codes?

13) What goals influenced the creation of different Manual English Codes?

14) What are pidgin languages?

15) What are creole languages?

Section 1 – ASL Linguistics
William Stokoe

Bill Stokoe was an English scholar who was offered a job to teach at Gallaudet College in the late 1950's. When he accepted the position he was expecting to focus his efforts on teaching Chaucer to deaf people but he soon discovered a very fascinating thing: the deaf students used a gestural form of communication that did not seem to follow the rules of English. Now curious about this gestural communication, Stokoe began to study it. He started asking questions and noticed that certain variations could be predicted depending on whether students were talking among themselves or with their teachers. Stokoe began to suspect that the gestural communication he was observing was in fact a language.

The idea that these gestures comprised a language was not readily accepted at Gallaudet. Even the deaf people did not believe that the gestures were anything more than an imperfect representation of English in the air. But Stokoe persisted. He attended a Summer-time linguistics institute and returned in the Fall full of ideas for scientifically testing his hypothesis.

The first challenge in identifying ASL as a language lay in determining its phonology: that is, the smallest parts which make up the language. Using movie cameras and black & white video, Stokoe started documenting this gestural communication. He then reviewed the material and discovered three of the primary features combined to create the signs. He called them the signation (sig), designator (dez), and the tabula (tab). Stokoe created the term "Cherology" in order to distinguish these parts of manual language parts from the study of spoken language parts (phonology).

In 1960 Stokoe published his first analysis: *Sign Language Structure*. In 1965 he and two deaf students at Gallaudet had published the *Dictionary of American Sign Language* (DASL). The DASL remains unique among ASL dictionaries: it is organized by the structure of ASL, not alphabetically upon the English words used to label the signs. In this sense it was the only true "dictionary" of ASL until a second was created in the late 1990's. Stokoe's dictionary is organized by locations, meaning that all signs near the face are together, signs which require both hands contacting each other are together, and so forth. For more than thirty years there was no other dictionary of ASL organized by how the signs are produced - all other "sign dictionaries" were simply lists of words or "lexicons."

Although he had published such carefully researched works, Stokoe faced great difficulties in having his research respected and understood at Gallaudet. The popular myth, influenced strongly by oralism, was that signs were no more than bad English on the hands, wholly unworthy of any serious scientific study. While other people around the nation started coming to Gallaudet to learn more about this "new" gestural language, the English department and other faculty members at Gallaudet (both deaf and hearing) felt embarrassed by Stokoe's work. They created the linguistics lab in order to get Stokoe out of the academic building. They wanted to send him off to the outer edge of campus since they thought his ideas were off center.

The linguistics lab thrived and researchers came from across the United States and also from around the world. They learned about the linguistics of ASL. Some further developed our current understanding of the structure and use of ASL, such as James Woodward, Nancy Frishberg, and Robbin Battison, who identified palm orientation as the fourth essential parameter of signs. Many international researchers returned to their homes and started analyzing the signed languages from their own countries. More deaf people started to pursue a scientific understanding of their own language. The linguistics lab (which had been created to get Stokoe, who had tenure, out of the English department) had become a center for international signed language research.

Because of the established traditions of spoken language research, few linguistics journals were willing to publish research on signed languages. In 1972, Stokoe started publishing Sign Language Studies (SLS) in order to provide a focused forum specifically on signed language linguistics. The journal focused largely on American Sign Language and its first twenty years of publication contain nearly every significant study on the structure and use of American Sign Language. During that time the major linguistic journals began to accept more and more work on ASL as mainstream linguistic work. The result upon SLS was that it became a forum for more research on signed languages from other countries, allowing an improved understanding of the similarities and differences of signed languages around the world.

1955	1960	1965	1972
Stokoe begins teaching at Gallaudet College	Stokoe publishes first research on ASL	Stokoe publishes the Dictionary of ASL	Stokoe begins publishing Sign Language Studies

Figure 4.1 - William Stokoe's Milestones

In 1985, Bill Stokoe retired from Gallaudet but continued to edit SLS. The linguistics lab had grown to a three-part entity during his tenure at Gallaudet: the linguistics lab, the linguistics department, and the linguistics library. When Bill left in 1985, however, Gallaudet University closed down everything but the linguistics department. Since it had all been created to keep Bill Stokoe busy and out of the way, it wasn't needed anymore now that Stokoe had retired. While the resources were valuable, they truly weren't needed anymore because by 1985 ASL research had become a common topic for doctoral dissertations and publications in mainstream linguistics journals.

Stokoe, even in retirement, still demonstrated significant commitment to ASL research by continuing to edit and contribute to Sign Language Studies and also through his Linstok Press. He died on April 4th, 2000 at the age of 80. William Stokoe had planted the seed for linguistic research around the world on signed languages and he is remembered fondly by the Deaf community.

In any language community there will be variety of how the language is used with other people. There are many factors that influence these varieties such as age, gender, and the relative status of the people communicating. Everyone has their own idiosyncrasies in how they use their language including different ways of talking with different kinds of people. The changes in how we talk can include the way we pronounce our words, which words we use, what we mean by our words, and even what kind of word orders we use. When we communicate with children or foreigners, we tend to use the most basic patterns of our language with them because we assume that they will not understand the more complicated patterns of our language. In English we may take a sentence such as "John was delivered the summons last night" and convey it very differently to a non-native user of English: "The police gave John a paper last night. The paper says that John must go to a court of law." Every language on earth has rules that allow transformations from basic sentence patterns to more complex sentences (and back again).

The History of Language Variety in ASL

In American Sign Language there is also variety in how the language can be used. When ASL was first being seriously studied by William Stokoe in the late 1950's, he noticed that his deaf students signed very differently with him than they did among themselves. Stokoe first labeled this difference Diglossia, which is a linguistic term for when a community uses one form of language for everyday interaction (the "low" form) and another form of language for official interaction (the "high" form).

Since the time that Stokoe started his research, there has been a growing understanding of the complexity of ASL, the general rules for producing words, ordering words, and the shades of meaning that those words convey. It is important to understand that ASL did have rules prior to the 1960s. An effort began in 1913 to document and preserve American Sign Language on film. These historic films demonstrate the rules of ASL long before the language was ever subjected to linguistic analysis. Clearly, the language was flourishing long before 1913. There are records of the existence of signed languages used among deaf people[12] prior to 1817 – the year that the United States of America witnessed the opening of its first permanent school for deaf children[13]. Hartford, Connecticut was where deaf students from across New England interacted with their teacher, Laurent Clerc, a deaf man from France.[14] Clerc was tri-lingual (at least) knowing French Sign Language, French, and English. He would become influential in the future of American Sign Language as his sign language and those of his students merged into post-1817 American Sign Language.[15]

Although the written and filmed records document the history of ASL, no one would make use of them as research tools until Stokoe began to investigate it. Soon after Stokoe's first publications – and as the deaf community was beginning to consider ASL as a bonafide language – a separate movement was also taking place which sought to expand the use of ASL as a tool for teaching English. This movement began in the 1960's and initially sought to borrow ASL words in an attempt to combine them with English syntax. This resulted in several manual English codes. The development of these codes and the continued exploration of American Sign Language created a need to distinguish between the signing styles that reflected the natural grammar of American Sign Language and the signing styles that did not reflect a natural signed language but rather reflected the encoding of English.

In the midst of this attempt to delineate language from code came an observation of language variation first noted by William Stokoe and then expanded upon by James Woodward. Stokoe had noticed that his students would structure their sign production

---

[12] Particularly the Deaf community on Martha's Vineyard, Massachusetts.

[13] We covered this in Unit One... remember?

[14] And if the students who came from Martha's vineyard had not been in Clerc's first class, ASL might have ended up being a lot more similar to French Sign Language. The differences between the two languages appear to have their origins in the influence of the Deaf students who already had a signed language: Martha's Vineyard Sign Language.

[15] After Clerc's students had influenced Clerc's ASL and Clerc had modified his own signing, At this point Clerc was *quadralingual*.

one way when they talked with him and another way when they communicated with each other. Stokoe called this difference "diglossia", meaning two languages. One "language" being used in formal, educational settings, and the other being used for informal or casual conversation.

James Woodward, a researcher who worked with Stokoe, studied this variation in language use and gave it the title "Pidgin Sign English" commonly known by the acronym PSE. Woodward felt that the signing that happened between deaf and hearing people was less than a full-fledged language and was the result of ASL users and English users trying to get by with something in between.

Once linguists began to investigate spoken pidgin languages more extensively, it became clear that the term "pidgin" does not describe the interaction between deaf and hearing people that Woodward was describing. True pidgins develop when people who do not share a common language (many "low" languages) make attempts to communicate with each other through a language of power or authority (one "high" language). One clear example of the use of pidgins is among African slaves (who spoke many different languages) attempting to communicate with each other through the language of their captors, for example, Portuguese. This resulted in a spontaneous form of communication that could develop over time but would generally remain dependent on reduced, basic forms without complex sentences. With only two languages involved between deaf and hearing people, and with the hearing person knowing the majority (or "high") language, it is impossible for a pidgin to develop. Woodward later apologized for introducing the term "Pidgin Sign English," but this term would remain for decades as the most commonly used to describe the use of ASL signs in English word order.

A few years after the creation of the term "PSE", Dennis Cokely suggested that this interaction was really "Learner's Grammar" and "Foreigner Register." This meant that the hearing people who were learning to sign depended heavily on the grammar of their native language (English) while the deaf people simplified their language (ASL) to accommodate people who did not know their language well.

During research in the late 1980's, Ceil Lucas and Clayton Valli discovered that deaf people also use different varieties of ASL among themselves and that some deaf people used the same varieties of signing with hearing people as they did with other deaf people. Lucas and Valli identified the mix of ASL and English features as "Contact Signing" (or CS). Contact communication results from people who use two different languages coming in contact with each other. Lucas and Valli identified a variety of ASL and English features which generally identified Contact Signing.

Stokoe's Research on Variation

William Stokoe (1960) first introduced the idea of a single line representing "possible communication behavior of American deaf persons" which would have "... at one end a completely normal American English exchange, the 'listener' with perfect lip reading ability receiving all that the speaker with perfect articulation is saying. At the opposite end would be a completely visual exchange, the 'speaker' and the 'hearer' using only a system of gesture, facial expression, and manual configurations as symbols. Of course, neither end is reached in actuality." (p 31)

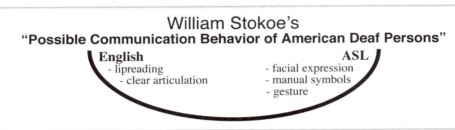

William Stokoe's
"Possible Communication Behavior of American Deaf Persons"

Figure 4.2 - Possible Communication Components

But as soon as Stokoe proposes this representation of communication in the deaf community, he immediately dismisses it: "... the actually observed communication is a combinations in all degrees of these two, with or without vocal, whispered, or silent articulation as supplement or accompaniment." (p 32)

Stokoe first noted variety in ASL in his 1960 monograph and suggested that the level of bilingualism in the signer may influence their language use: "Presumably their language habits will be more or less affected by the extent to which English is their second language...but two languages that can be used simultaneously (at least at a word level) may be more strongly drawn into syntactical conformity" (p 80, parenthesis in original)

William Stokoe's
"Observed Communication Behavior of American Deaf Persons"

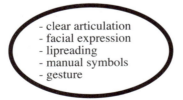

Figure 4.3 - Observed Communication Components

Stokoe formally proposed that Ferguson's description of diglossia be applied to the language variation in the deaf community where English structures influenced the ordering of ASL signs in formal, or "high" situations where less English structures appeared in informal, or "low" situations. The problem that remains with this attempt at defining formal ASL and informal ASL as diglossia is the fact that there is still only one language being used: ASL. Ferguson's concept requires two different languages. It is not enough to suggest that one language (English) might influence the structure of another (ASL) in formal settings. Ferguson's concept of diglossia cannot adequately describe this kind of variation in ASL.

Woodward's Research on Variation

James Woodward mentioned diglossia in 1972 and suggested ways of studying it as it related to ASL. In that same article he mentioned what he then called "pidgin sign English" as the resulting communication of signing and speaking at the same time. Thus from Woodward's *initial* article, "pidgin sign English" referred only to the mixture of language that occurred from combining two communication modes simultaneously: signs and speech. Woodward was still using the term "diglossia" to describe how the setting and topic influenced language use in the Deaf community. He suggested that ASL and American English occupied different ends of a "diglossic scale". The figure below shows the two ends of such a diglossic scale, one end showing that formal situations were closely tied to English while informal settings were identified as ASL.

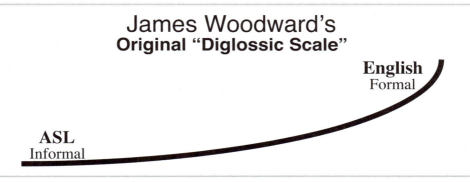

James Woodward's
Original "Diglossic Scale"

English
Formal

ASL
Informal

Figure 4.4 - ASL & English Diglossia

Woodward's original definition of "pidgin sign English" would be the combination of speaking English while signing ASL and could appear anywhere on the line between ASL and English in the above chart. A point on the line closer to the ASL side would imply less (incomplete) English speech while signing ASL. A point on the line closer to the English side would imply less (incomplete) ASL signing while speaking English.

Within one year, however, Woodward would officially coin the acronym "PSE" and publish a formal, although preliminary, description of it. Within this 1973 paper Woodward acknowledged that research on and definitions of Pidgin and Creole languages were still in development. Woodward then described "PSE" as having the following characteristics: 1) Articles, such as "a", "an," or "the" in English may or may not be used; but if used typically they are spellings of the English words "A" and "T-H-E". 2) Plurality by reduplication (an ASL feature) may or may not be used; but using a suffix such as the letter "s" (an English feature) is not generally used. 3) Use of English words such as "is", "am," or "are" (not a feature of ASL) is generally represented by a single ASL sign commonly glossed as TRUE. 4) Progressive aspect (an ASL feature) is sometimes maintained by reduplicating the verb. 5) Perfective aspect (an ASL feature) is also sometimes maintained through the use of the sign commonly glossed as FINISH (Woodward noted that "PSE" users tend to use a specific variety of this sign which is more restricted in general ASL usage, but he did not describe exactly what those differences were). It is interesting to note that all five of these characteristics of "PSE" are represented by elements of ASL. In other words, already existing components of ASL are being utilized to represent information in ways that parallel English language structures. This raises the question: *If every element of "PSE" already exists within ASL, then how is "PSE" different than ASL?* Woodward and Stokoe had noticed something very real, but their attempts to describe it as something other than variation within ASL has lead to significant misunderstanding and division within the Deaf community. The figure below represents Woodward's descriptions of "PSE" as the use of ASL elements.

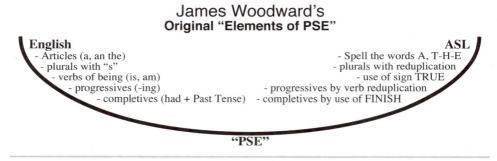

James Woodward's
Original "Elements of PSE"

English	ASL
- Articles (a, an the)	- Spell the words A, T-H-E
- plurals with "s"	- plurals with reduplication
- verbs of being (is, am)	- use of sign TRUE
- progressives (-ing)	- progressives by verb reduplication
- completives (had + Past Tense)	- completives by use of FINISH

"PSE"

Figure 4.5 - "PSE" Composed of ASL Elements

In another 1973 paper, Woodward refers to the diglossic scale of his 1972 article as "a continuum of language varieties between ASL and Manual English"; but in truth, the 1972 article did not indicate that this continuum moved between two manual forms – he had indicated that it was a mix of signing ASL and speaking English at the same time. This represents a sudden shift in the research of how English is used by the Deaf community and may reflect rapid developments and changes of thought in signed language research in the early 1970s. The problem is that these two different representations of language variation do not completely overlap. While both suggest that the language of ASL occupies one end of the continuum, the other end is either occupied by 1) a spoken language - American English, or by 2) a manual representation of the language - "Manual English". The first (1972) continuum moves between two *languages* and *at the same time* it moves across two different *modalities* (signed verses spoken/written). It really is too much to have one line represent two variables (languages and modalities) of difference. The second (1973) continuum maintains a *single modality* (signing) but moves between language (ASL) and an *invented encoding* of language ("Manual English"). In the 1972 model, "PSE" represents the use of two modalities at the same time - simultaneous communication. In the 1973 model, "PSE" represents signing with influences of both "Manual English" (which Woodward does not clearly define) and

ASL – Woodward is no longer making any mention about simultaneous productions of ASL signs and spoken English.

How do Deaf People Represent English?

There have been many manual inventions for representing English to Deaf people. Deaf people have been involved in the creation of some of these systems. Several of these systems will be discussed later in this chapter. It is important to note, however, that the Deaf community has long made use of many different ways to represent English among themselves. Among the many visual ways that English is represented and used by Deaf adults are the following:

- Writing and Reading
- Fingerspelling
- The visual remnants of spoken language (speech reading)
- The modification of ASL signs to include fingerspelling handshapes for key elements of the English word

Stokoe's and Woodward's research explored these variables. Deaf people are able to represent English in a variety of ways, but this does not necessarily mean that the result is another language or anything other than "using ASL to represent English".

Other Research on Variation

Reilly and McIntire (1980) noted that "PSE" utilized many English structures for creating complex sentences that are atypical of pidgin languages in general. Dennis Cokely (1983, 1984) reassessed the issue of "PSE" by first reviewing what had become more complete definitions of both pidgins and the process of pidginization. Cokely concluded that the phenomenon described by Woodward does not legitimately constitute a pidgin, even though some of the elements of pidginization are evident. Specifically Cokely proposed that these varieties of ASL constitute attempts by hearing learners of ASL to communicate which are then assessed by deaf people as "learner's grammar" (which may include errors, over generalizations of ASL and influences of English). The deaf people then respond by using a reduced form of ASL or "foreigner register" which is used to assist communication with people not yet fluent in the target language. While Cokely's explanation may not include all instances of "PSE", it does place the language use clearly as part of ASL, not a separate entity lost somewhere between two languages.

Ceil Lucas and Clayton Valli (1992) extensively researched this area and found significant variety in what they call "Contact Signing". They not only found instances of Contact Signing between most (although not all) interactions of deaf and hearing people, but they also found instances of Contact Signing in some interactions of Deaf people with other Deaf people. Their analysis indicates that Contact Signing consists of the use of ASL that generally avoids the use of many complex ASL elements (such as nonmanual negation, aspectual inflection, conditionals, rhetorical questions, and topicalization) while including some basic elements of English (such as mouthing of English words, use of uniquely English word order, conjunctions, and prepositions). Lucas and Valli emphasized that these results came from contact between the two languages of English and ASL and did not constitute an otherwise natural variety of ASL.

Again, it is interesting to note that nearly all of the documented elements of English were produced using components already present within ASL. The single exception is of the word orders unique to English (some may argue that the use of mouth movements come only from English, yet mouth movements along with facial expression are significant components of ASL). While the result is clearly influenced by English, only certain parts of syntax seem inherently limited to English. In other words, all the elements composing the signs themselves exist within the confines of American Sign Language, only some of the word orders seem to be uniquely influenced by English. The figure below represents this interaction.

Figure 4.6 – ASL & English Influencing Contact Signing

Ceil Lucas and Clayton Valli (1992) identified a number of features that appear in Contact Signing. The chart below identifies those features from each language (ASL and English) that were used and those which were apparently avoided, or not used.

English Features Used	English Features NOT Used	ASL Features Used	ASL Features NOT Used
Conjunctions (and, because, but)	Verbs + prepositions (go with, look at)	Agreement Verbs (subject / object)	Aspect Inflection (duration, intensity)
English mouth patterns	Relative Clauses	Signs without mouthing	Topicalization
Prepositions	Comparative "more"		ASL Determiners (indexing/pointing)
English order (?)	Determiners (the, this, that)		ASL word order (?)
Subordinate clauses	Modal Constructions (can, must, etc)		Role Shifting

Figure 4.7 – ASL and English Features of Contact Signing

The use of *topicalization* (emphasizing a subject or object by placing it at the beginning of a sentence) and of *body shifting* for role, comparisons or conditionals were two important components which appeared to distinguish ASL signing from Contact signing. These features are more complex aspects of ASL and are generally learned later by children acquiring ASL. They are therefore not *basic* elements of ASL but mark advanced grammatical features of ASL.

A Revised Model of Variation in ASL

These explorations of variety in ASL and influences of English upon some of these varieties are represented in the following model of language interaction between ASL and English. This model reflects both modalities (signing and speaking) and both languages (ASL and English).

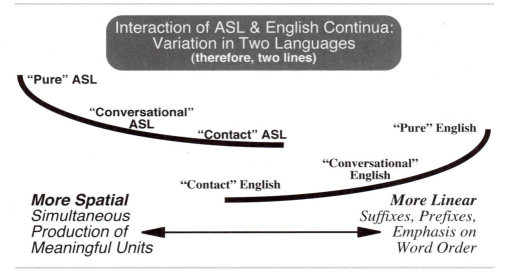

Figure 4.8 – Bilingual / Bimodal Language Contact

This model recognizes the fact that not only two different languages are in contact (ASL and English) but also two different channels / modalities (signing and speaking). The main components of the model are two distinct lines: one for speech information, the other for signed information. Each line represents more complex grammatical structures at their extreme ends and the most simple or basic grammatical structures toward the middle. For example, the signing line has more complex grammatical ASL on the left side but has contact signing that can be correlated to English structures on the right-hand side.

In the lower portions of each modality continua are the most basic structures of ASL and English, which for both languages are simple Subject-Verb or Subject-Verb-Object sentences. Since both sentence patterns appear in both languages, it is physically possible to utter complete sentences in both languages at the same time. Some people may argue that mouth movement patterns reflecting complete English words are an indication that the rules of ASL are not being followed. It is true that certain aspects of ASL require specific mouth movement patterns which are not related to English speech patterns, however, much of ASL *vocabulary* does not require specific mouth movement patterns.

During normal productions of grammatical spoken English it is entirely possible to keep one's hands completely immobile; it's also possible to produce grammatical English while continuously gesturing. Hand movement does not indicate whether English is being used or not, but certainly some hand movements can play a significant role in the clarity of the message (a classic example is the use of hand gestures to clarify the use of phrases such as "that one" or "this item"). Whether the hands produce ASL signs or simple gestures does not determine whether an accompanying spoken message is English or not. Likewise, the movement of the lips alone cannot determine whether an accompanying signed message is ASL or not.

It is therefore physically possible to simultaneously produce a signed message which follows the rules of ASL while also producing a spoken message which follows the rules of English. Just because it is physically possible, however, does not mean that it happens very often. The best chance of following the rules of both languages simultaneously requires using only the most basic structures in each language – most likely two-word or three-word sentences. It is actually more likely that attempting to use both languages at the same time would generate some amount of ungrammatical nonsense in one or both languages at the same time. The production of true "Simultaneous Communication" is rarely grammatical and is likely to shift into sentence structures of either Contact Signing or Contact Speaking if any word orders other than SV or SVO are attempted.

Moving along the more complex end of the Contact Signing line means that ASL signs are being used in sentence patterns unique to English and therefore require a shared knowledge of ASL and English by both the presenter and the receiver in order to be effective for communication. If speech occurs simultaneously, then this is considered Sign Supported Speech (after Johnson, Liddell & Erting, 1989) because the mode containing the more linguistically complete message is the spoken modality and the signs serve mostly to support the spoken message. In contrast, Speech Supported Sign may occur when a complete ASL message co-occurs with elements of spoken English. Spoken English following the rules of ASL grammar has yet to be intensively studied but its existence has been noted as "CODA speak" (Jacobs, 1992; B. Schick, personal communication) in which hearing children of deaf adults (CODAs) use their knowledge of two languages to produce spoken utterances of English words, often with non-standard pronunciations which represent the manners in which their deaf parents may have pronounced the English words.

Linear ASL and Spatial ASL

Given our understanding that the basic word orders of English and ASL are both Subject + Verb + Object, and that many Deaf people use what Bernard Bragg has called "Englished ASL" among themselves, there is no particular reason to try to identify this form of ASL use as being a language other than ASL. While it may be that English influences the variation from time to time, it would be more consistent to use labels which clarify the kind of ASL signing being produced: *Linear ASL* (grammatically simple ASL) and *Spatial ASL* (grammatically complex ASL). **Linear ASL** makes less use of inflections, dual articulations, non-manual markers, and grammatical or indexical space. **Spatial ASL** would make more use of these same features. These varieties of ASL (linear vs spatial) are not discrete and precise, but rather general terms which help us to define where a certain kind of signing or speaking falls along the continua of language varieties. For example, the English sentence "I asked him 'Did you give it to her?'" can be produced with a *single sign* properly inflected with appropriate eye gaze, eye brow position, body posture, handshape, orientation, movement and locations. Such use of ASL would very clearly be an example of Spatial ASL. The same concepts could be represented by thirteen signs (including fingerspelling) so that the sequence of ASL signs matches the word order of the English sentence – an example of Linear ASL. Most everyday use of ASL is likely to be between these two extremes, so the labels merely identify an overall *tendency* for a person to sign (or to understand) one style or the other.

Section 2 –Language Choice & Variation in the Deaf Community
Oral Communication and the Deaf Community

As we learned earlier, the Milan Conference of 1880 had a profound effect on the methodology of teaching deaf children around the world for more than a century. Many schools to this day remain proponents of pure oralism, which excludes any use of signed language, and often excludes any forms of gestural communication as well. Although there is now a greater variety of choices for educational philosophies and communication options for deaf children, the decisions still reside with the parents and not the Deaf children.

The Milan Conference stated outright opposition to signed languages, effectively banning them from public life for all deaf people. The manualists who opposed these strict oralists did not hold such an extreme view in their own opposition. Very few (if any) manualists proposed banning the use of spoken language or lipreading skills. In fact, Edward Miner Gallaudet called his communication philosophy at Gallaudet College the "Combined Method" which provided for the use of signed language for instruction, but also supported the use of lipreading and speech production for those deaf students who exhibited promise in developing these skills. Gallaudet believed that the primary error of the oral method was its all-or-nothing-at-all approach.

The oppression that resulted from the Milan Conference has resulted in significant distrust of oral-only educators and a strong resistance to oralism as an educational option for deaf children. Yet the fact remains that for some deaf children, the oral methods do work. Many of these children are only moderately deaf (culturally referred to as "Hard of Hearing"). Some of them may succeed in oral education, but they also learn to distrust the use of signed languages. Many orally successful students are taught that they became successful because they were not exposed to signed languages. Such indoctrination leads to further division within the Deaf community. There is no evidence to support this idea and these deaf children would have most likely achieved at least the same proficiency in spoken language had they also been exposed to signed language.

Very few deaf adults find themselves in situations where they would find no benefit from speechreading skills. Some deaf adults depend on speechreading to the exclusion of any signing, while many deaf adults, being bilingual in ASL and English, depend upon speechreading as a significant tool for their interaction with people who are not deaf.

Just as there is variety in the ability to speechread, there is also variety in the ability of deaf people to speak intelligibly. Many late-deafened people retain their ability to speak but find they have no gift whatsoever for speechreading. This sets them up for mostly one-way communication and they may either dominate conversations or limit their questions to those with "yes" or "no" answers. Some deaf people find that when they attempt to use their voices they are no longer treated as intelligent people. People who are not deaf often confuse deaf speech patterns with the speech patterns of mental retardation. People who have cerebral palsy or who are aphasiac after having a stroke find similar frustrations because people will associate their limited ability to speak to mean a limited intelligence. Some deaf people will therefore chose not to use their voices at all in order to encourage the use of completely visual communication through written language or gestures.

The choices and preferences of each individual deaf person need to be respected. It can be just as oppressive to sign to a deaf person who rejects signing as it would be to force a deaf person to lipread rather than use a signed language, gestures, or a written language. There are multiple ways to communicate in the Deaf community, just as there are multiple ways to communicate in the community of people who are not deaf. It is important to remember people's communication preferences and work together rather than forcing one person's preferences upon another.

The DeafBlind Community

There are some deaf people who also have vision impairment or blindness. There is great variety of vision loss, just as there is great variety in hearing loss. This means that the exact services that a DeafBlind person will need will be different from person to person.

Some DeafBlind people may have been born both deaf and blind, some may have lost their sight before their hearing, some may have lost their hearing first, and other people may have become suddenly deaf and blind at the same time due to illness or injury. While the causes vary, they lead to similar needs for communication. For people who cannot see with any clarity and cannot hear well enough to access spoken language, they will require tactile communication of some kind. Depending on their background, they may prefer Braille, fingerspelling in the palm, block printing in the palm or on the arm, the use of block letters pressed against their skin, using a special alphabet glove with letters at designated locations, using sign language read tactually, or a special form of lipreading using the whole hand.

Most DeafBlind people who started out as deaf people and later lost their vision will prefer reading sign language if they learned signs before becoming blind. Engaging in tactile communication with these DeafBlind people requires some thought as to how grammatical information on the face is transferred to the hands. It also may require some modifications for sign productions and an awareness of what information is accessible to the DeafBlind person. If you are using only one hand to exchange tactile communication then some classifier constructions and certain two-handed signs may be misunderstood by the DeafBlind person since only one hand is receiving information.

Some DeafBlind people still have useable vision. They may have a vision loss that is stable or progressive. A progressive loss may be particularly frustrating to the DeafBlind person because just as they can deal with a certain degree of vision loss, it worsens to the point that they have to adjust all over again. People experiencing tunnel vision may need to sit *at a distance* from the interpreter in order to have the entire signing space in their visual field, then change to being right in front of the interpreter tracking hand movement by placing their hands on the wrists of the interpreter, and finally change to placing their hands on the interpreter's hands when vision alone no longer provides useful information. Remember to work with the DeafBlind person to respect their preferences. It may seem counter-intuitive, but they may need to sit further away in order to see you clearly. They may not know signed language and require fingerspelling or even palm printing (using your finger to trace the shapes of letters into their hand).

Communicating with DeafBlind people requires consideration of environmental sights. How many people are in the room? Who are they? When interacting with deaf people we know the deaf person can see just who we are, but the DeafBlind person cannot make that determination so easily. We must identify ourselves when we start our communication. We may also find ourselves providing guide services entering or leaving a room, or just moving around in an environment. If the DeafBlind person is familiar with the environment already, these services may not be needed. In fact we can make matters worse by moving furniture if the DeafBlind person knew where it used to be but now does not know it has been moved to. In a new environment, perhaps a good description of the room's layout will suffice. Often it is just easier to guide the DeafBlind person through the environment, especially if both the interpreter and the DeafBlind person need to move to a new location together.

While some DeafBlind people may resent their condition, they are generally pleased to have people who take the time to communicate with them. It is important to be open and honest with the DeafBlind person at all times. Often DeafBlind people will be able to provide helpful solutions if any problems come up.

Orin Cornett and Cued Language Transliteration

The 1960's saw a flurry of activity regarding deaf people. The rubella epidemic was causing thousands of children to be born deaf if their mothers had been sick with German measles during their pregnancies. William Stokoe had determined that ASL was a full-fledged language rather than a form of English-on-the-hands. A group of educators in California had convened to discuss how to use signs to convey English (now that they knew it was not English-on-the-hands). Meanwhile, a professor of physics at Gallaudet was alarmed at the numbers of deaf children who had poor English comprehension scores.

Dr. Orin Cornett learned of the difficulties that deaf children had with reading when he read a government report that found most deaf high school students were reading at only a third-grade level. Cornett began searching for ways that would expose deaf children to the sounds of spoken language without the ambiguity of lipreading. After investigating fingerspelling and the Dutch "Mouth/Hand" system, he devised what he called Cued Speech, in 1966. Eight handshapes and four locations combine with the normal lip movements of spoken language to reveal the speech sounds being made without ambiguity. In this way, deaf children can visually access the sounds of spoken language and become native users of the same language that their parents use.

While Cornett's creation has had a tremendous impact upon the language development of thousands of deaf children, the deaf community has resisted cueing largely because of the way Orin Cornett promoted his creation. Orin Cornett had not worked with the deaf community, nor was he greatly aware of deaf culture and the pride associated with American Sign Language. Although Cornett created cueing primarily as a literacy tool, he believed that the use of cues would also enhance speech-reading and speech clarity among deaf children. He promoted Cued Speech as "the answer" to thousands of hearing parents who wished for their children to be hearing children. In this way, Cornett promised more than his creation could deliver.

Research has demonstrated that cueing works as a literacy tool for deaf children. Unfortunately there are many people who have been mislead by the name into thinking that its sole purpose is to focus on speaking and speech-reading skills. Cueing has not been shown to improve speaking abilities nor to improve speech-reading abilities. Critics of the system point out that too few people know cues and that once the child grows up, there is no support system for deaf kids who only communicate through cues. This criticism assumes that no other means of communication can be used alongside the use of cues.

The important point that is so often overlooked is that cueing represents spoken languages sufficiently for deaf children to attain internalized native ability in them. This has a direct effect upon reading and writing abilities and it is here that the value of cued-language transliteration is most evident. Research indicates that deaf children who regularly use cueing are not merely at grade-level with their hearing peers, but are in fact above grade-level with regards to reading and writing. Because Cued Speech has a minimal impact upon speech, but a major impact upon reading and general language knowledge, it is better referred to as Manual Cues or Cued Language.

Teachers of Deaf children are always faced with the problem of teaching their students to read. So many mainstream programs offer forms of signed codes for English as the primary mode of communication. This has resulted largely in deaf children who are semilingual - possessing inadequate skills in both ASL and English. Many schools for the deaf employ hearing teachers who use signs, yet know little about ASL. Many parents of deaf children are learning signs to communicate with their children, but remain ignorant of the intricacies, the grammar, the correct use of ASL. This promotes confusion among deaf children by reducing their exposure to fluent language models.

A common approach to bilingual/bicultural education is to ensure that Deaf children are educated by Deaf teachers through ASL. English lessons are explained in ASL and focus on written English. This view of English usage is limiting because spoken English and written English are very different in register variation and in contextual use. As a result, written English does not represent the full picture of English-speaking culture. Word play and rhyme are not conveyed accurately with written language forms. Intonation variation, puns, and the subtleties of human interaction (these are important aspects of culture) are not adequately conveyed in written forms. While these programs may indeed be bilingual, they are not adequately bicultural.

Most educational programs for deaf children that implemented Cued Language did so in exclusion of other means of communication, particularly American Sign Language. This is a significant reason that so many members of the deaf community have opposed cueing. Today, however, the proponents of cueing are working to employ cues side by side with American Sign Language within bilingual/bicultural educational programs. As more truly bilingual and bicultural programs are established in the United States and Canada, cued-language transliteration will become even more widespread.

By exposing the Deaf child to the intricacies of spoken language consistently and without ambiguity, cueing provides them with the same ability as their hearing peers to learn how to read. There is no reason for parents to avoid learning signs to communicate with their deaf child, but it is not realistic to expect the majority of parents with deaf children to become fluent models of American Sign Language. Because cueing is a finite encoding tool of eight handshapes and four locations, parents can easily learn the system in a matter of hours. As they begin communicating to their child they need only think about how to encode the spoken language that they already know. This allows the deaf child to be raised with fluent language models, as long as the parents work to improve their facility with the encoding tool.

Examples of Cueing

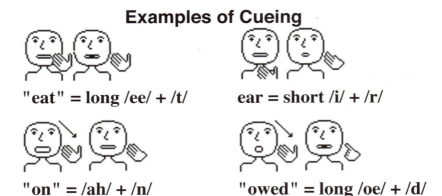

"eat" = long /ee/ + /t/   ear = short /i/ + /r/

"on" = /ah/ + /n/   "owed" = long /oe/ + /d/

The Cueing system represents 25 consonant sounds by combining mouth configurations with 8 handshapes:

Handshape 1 =

/d/   /zh/   /p/

Handshape 2 =

/Th/   /k/   /v/   /z/

Handshape 3 =

/h/   /r/   /s/

Handshape 4 =

/b/   /hw/   /n/

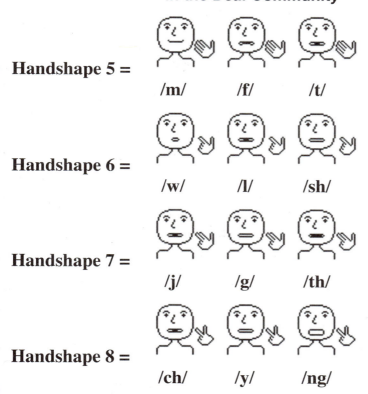

Handshape 5 =   /m/   /f/   /t/

Handshape 6 =   /w/   /l/   /sh/

Handshape 7 =   /j/   /g/   /th/

Handshape 8 =   /ch/   /y/   /ng/

The Cueing system represents 14 vowel sounds by combining mouth configuration with 4 locations:

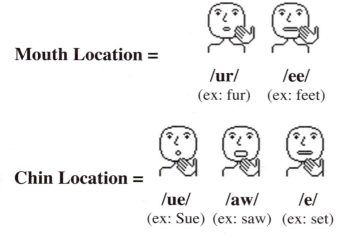

Mouth Location =   /ur/   /ee/
(ex: fur)   (ex: feet)

Chin Location =   /ue/   /aw/   /e/
(ex: Sue)   (ex: saw)   (ex: set)

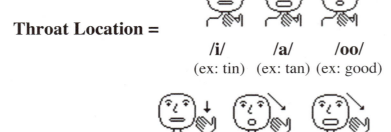

Throat Location =

/i/   /a/   /oo/

(ex: tin) (ex: tan) (ex: good)

Side Location:

/uh/   /oe/   /ah/

(ex: duh) (ex: toe)   (ex: aha)

The Cueing system represents vowel combinations (diphthongs) by combining the vowel configurations.

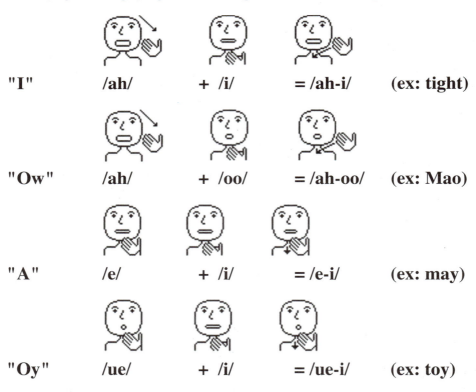

"I"	/ah/	+ /i/	= /ah-i/	(ex: tight)
"Ow"	/ah/	+ /oo/	= /ah-oo/	(ex: Mao)
"A"	/e/	+ /i/	= /e-i/	(ex: may)
"Oy"	/ue/	+ /i/	= /ue-i/	(ex: toy)

Cues are combined into Consonant + Vowel segments

Single syllable

The word "chew" or "choo" would be produced as a single combination of handshape 8 at the chin location while saying the sounds /chue/.

Repeated Syllable

The word "choo-choo" would be produced as a repeated combination of handshape 8 at the chin location while saying the sounds /chue/ /chue/.

Initial Vowel Syllable

The word "achoo!" (the English word for the sound a sneeze makes) would be produced in two parts. The first part would place the 5 handshape at the throat location while saying the sound /a/. The second part would be the combination of handshape 8 at the chin location while saying the sounds /chue/.

Final Consonant Syllable

The word "choose!" would be produced in two parts. The first part would be the combination of handshape 8 at the chin location while saying the sounds /chue/. The second part would produce handshape 2 at the side location while saying the sound /z/.

Diphthong Examples

/t/ + /I/ + /m/

The spoken English words "time" and "thyme" would both be represented the same way.

/m/ + /I/ + /t/

The spoken English words "might" and "mite" would both be represented the same way.

Computer Assisted Notetaking

Computer Assisted Notetaking, or CAN, is a form of transliteration that takes spoken English discourse and processes it into written English notes. The exact product can vary depending on the needs of the consumer. Computer Assisted Notetaking is different from Computer Assisted Real-time Transcription (CART). CAN requires the CANer to listen to the source text and understand its meaning, then produce condensed notes or headlines of information. CART requires a person trained in Court Reporting techniques to encode spoken language phonemically into a computer that then transliterates the encoded information into written language. CAN can be done on any computer with word-processing software while CART requires specific equipment and/or software in conjunction with a computer.

While it is possible for people trained in typing alone to provide CAN services, their training does not generally include message processing. This can result in notes which begin verbatim for the first sentence, but do not complete the sentence, then begin verbatim again with the third sentence because the typist missed the second sentence, and so on. This leads to very confusing notes without cohesion. True CANing requires the typist to process the information and determine the meaning. Faster typists can stay closer to the original words and phrases, but even slower typists can still produce very useful notes.

CART training, on the other hand, may require as much as two years of intensive training to learn the transcription system and gain enough speed to produce it consistently and accurately. As a result of this intensive training requirement, and the cost of special equipment or software, CART services are likely to cost more than CAN services, but will produce a more exact record of communication than CAN.

Either service can use electronic networks to connect remote viewing screens so that any number of people can access the service. Of course, the more video terminals used, the more expensive the entire service becomes. Often CANing is done with a laptop computer with the CANer and the consumer sitting side by side reading from the same screen.

The consumers of CAN are most likely late-deafened adults who have extensive knowledge of the majority spoken language around them. They most often do not know a signed language well enough to make use of it for interpreting services and may even be embarrassed by their deafness. Some consumers may be embarrassed by their deafness to the point that they wish the CANer to work separately from the consumer and use a network connection from the CANer's computer to the consumer's computer in order to give the appearance that it is the consumer who is taking their own notes. Sometimes this same arrangement will be preferred regardless of the consumer's feelings about deafness, such as when the CANer can function as official notetaker/secretary of proceedings and be seated next to the presenters while the network connection allows the consumer to participate as an audience member.

Ethical considerations for either service remain similar to those considerations for providing other interpreting or transliterating services. The information gained while working must remain confidential. The CANer or CARTer must remain faithful to the information without inserting personal biases or opinions. The CANer or CARTer should carefully consider their qualifications to adequately provide services in each communication event. Unlike interpreting, CAN and CART can produce permanent documents that can then be edited. These documents must remain the property of the people who did the communicating. Some CANer's will offer to edit and "clean up" any errors that occurred for an additional fee, but ultimately the information belongs to the communicators. CANed proceedings can sometimes serve as minutes for meetings or as other official documentation of an event. This is one of the main advantages to CANing or CARTing over other forms of interpreting or transliteration.

Manual English Codes, Pidgins & Creoles

In January of 1969 a group of people gathered in Southern California. They were concerned about the English language development in deaf children. 1960 had seen the first publication that gave linguistic consideration to American Sign Language. 1965 saw the first dictionary of ASL published. In 1965 came another publication: the Babbidge report, which stated that "the average graduate of a public residential school for the deaf... has an eighth grade education." (Babbidge, 1965). This report motivated Dr. Orin Cornette to develop cued speech as a means of exposing deaf children to spoken language from the most basic level of language: phonemes, or speech sounds.

It was the same report that motivated this group of people who gathered in California. They were concerned with the English language development of deaf children and sought an organized, visibly clear way of presenting English to them. As discussions progressed three related systems were developed. Initially they agreed to use ASL vocabulary as the base for inventing additional vocabulary. Different handshapes could replace the standard ASL handshapes in order to expand a single sign to cover many English words with similar meanings. The groups started to divide, however, when the issues turned to representing English morphology as pieces of meaning or as syllables. One group wished to keep the system closer to ASL by using different signs when the meaning was clearly different while another wanted to establish one and only one sign for any given English root morpheme, regardless of the meaning. An example of this is the English word "Butterfly." ASL has a sign for the concept, but it is possible to recognize the words "Butter" and "Fly" even though the concept of flying butter has little to do with butterflies. Keeping a separate sign would reduce confusions about meanings, but re-using other signs that a child already knows would mean the child would not need to memorize how to spell so many words.

The group divided into three smaller groups. Dennis Wampler, a child of deaf adults and a teacher of deaf children, believed that the vocabulary should be represented using Stokoe's sign notation system instead of using pictures. Since few people are skilled at reading Stokoe's notation system, few people took the time to learn to read the descriptions of each sign. Wampler named his system the **Linguistics Of Visual English** (LOVE) but it was never widely implemented.

The two remaining groups did publish dictionaries with pictures. **David Anthony**, a deaf teacher of deaf children, had actually started his system on his own with his Masters Thesis in 1965. Anthony led the group which eventually called their system **Seeing Essential English** which is known as SEE 1. SEE 1 primarily assigns English morphemes and syllable strings a single sign which may convey accurate meaning in their primary sense, but will not in any secondary or idiomatic uses. Two common examples are the signs used for "butter" and for "fly" combined to represent the word "butterfly;" and the signs for the English words "car" and "pet" for the word "carpet." In this way it more closely represents English but still depends on mixing ASL and English together.

The remaining group included Gerilee Gustason (a deaf teacher of deaf children), Donna Pfetzing (an interpreter with a deaf child), and Ester Zawolkow (an interpreter with deaf parents). They established **Signing Exact English** (SEE 2). SEE 2 stays more morphologically true to the ASL meanings of signs but will add specific signs for prefixes and suffixes. As an example, the SEE 2 production of "going" would combine a sign for "go" and a sign for "ing." The SEE 2 signs for "looked" would combine a sign for "look" and a sign for past tense. One problem with this approach is that SEE 2 also adds this past-tense marker to irregular verbs such as the following English words: went, saw, sat, ate, drove, and bought. Using the same past tense sign implies that these words should be really be spelled "goed, seeed, sited, eated, drived, and buyed." SEE 2 attempts to maintain ASL morphology, but it does so at the expense of English morphology. The result is a mix of two languages, which represents neither language accurately. Figure 4.8 shows the three different Manual English Codes that came from David Anthony's original "Signing Essential English".

Figure 4.9 – Three Different Manual English Codes

Proponents of these systems suggest that they lead to improved acquisition or learning of English among deaf students, but this has not been strongly supported by research. The primary benefit of these codes is to parents, teachers, and interpreters who are not fluent in ASL. People who already know English can learn these codes fairly quickly, since the codes rely heavily on the syntax of English. People who are not fluent in ASL may use these codes as a means of communication with deaf children that would otherwise only be oral. The most significant result of the creation of manual English codes is that they opened the door for the use of signed languages in classrooms. After more than thirty-five years of pure oralism, signs were again permitted in some classrooms with deaf children.

With closer investigation, we can see that manual English codes are similar to pidgin languages. As we learned earlier in the discussion of language variation, pidgins develop as a mix of three or more languages. One of the languages is perceived as dominant and that one lends the vocabulary to the pidgin. The other languages contribute grammar and pronunciation rules. Pidgins develop where access to the target language is seriously restricted and where there are insufficient numbers of people fluent in any of the minority languages to use it for interpersonal communication.

These conditions for pidgin languages are exactly what surround the use of manual English codes. Contact signing is an ebb and flow between two languages (and can vary significantly depending on a person's fluency in each language); but manual English codes are more restricted. The three pieces, which come together for manual English codes, are 1) the use of ASL vocabulary (the dominant language), 2) the heavy dependence upon English syntax, and 3) the use of inventions to alter some vocabulary and to represent English grammatical morphemes. These inventions also alter the pronunciation of ASL signs as handshapes are changed from correct ASL forms to visually distinct forms.

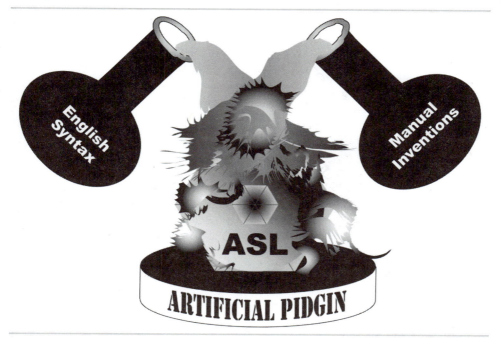

Figure 4.10 – Manual English Codes Are Not Languages

One of the more interesting features of this mix is that because the vocabulary items come from ASL, it means that ASL is the dominant language of the mixture, not English. Thus, manual English codes lead a child toward learning ASL more than they lead the child to learn English. Manual English codes were proposed as a means of allowing deaf students to be exposed to English visually; but instead the children are exposed to a mixture of languages. How can this mix of language and inventions result in students learning anything other than mixed language? The one aspect of English that remains unaltered through the use of manual English codes is the use of lip movements for English words. Those students who manage to succeed in learning English through exposure to manual English codes are most likely depending upon lip movements to consistently represent English.

Deaf children who are only exposed to a manual English code (which is an invented, or artificial, pidgin) will each develop their own creoles (Supalla, 1991). Creoles are the result of a natural process in which children adapt the imperfect language data of a pidgin as they acquire it and transform the pidgin into a new human language. The most significant danger of the use of invented pidgins is that the deaf children who creolize them within different school settings will end up creating different creoles. This creates significant variation in the language use of young deaf adults. This variation poses an even greater challenge for any interpreter working with different deaf people who all have their own mainstream creoles.

The transcommunication of spoken English to manual English codes (identified here as "Artificial Pidgins") and vice versa has traditionally been called "Transliterating." As we will see in Unit Six, this label should only be used to describe transcommunication work between two modes of the same language. Since Artificial Pidgins are not a language the term "Transliterating" is not technically accurate. Neither is term "Interpreting" is appropriate. The only appropriate label for this kind of work is the generic label of "Transcommunication."

Summary

This Unit presented the rich variety of communication preferences found within the Deaf community. William Stokoe's efforts helped to identify American Sign Language as a true and legitimate language. Stokoe also noted that there was variation in ASL, which seemed linked to English syntax. Lucas and Valli have identified such language interaction as Contact Signing. Various means of communicating exist within the deaf community including the use of signed languages, contact signing, manual cues, speech and speechreading, written language, and gestural language. DeafBlind people need accommodation, primarily based on communication preferences and providing access to visual information. The use of computer technology has recently been employed to allow for near-immediate access to information via written language. Finally, the creation of various manual English codes was reviewed, analyzed and compared to pidgins that deaf children naturally creolize into their own variations of ASL.

Section 1 Review Questions

1)   What year did William Stokoe publish "Sign Language Structure"?

2)   What significance did "Sign Language Structure" have regarding ASL research?

3)   What was the name of Stokoe's dictionary?

4)   What made Stokoe's dictionary a true dictionary as opposed to being a mere lexicon?

5)   What was the name of Stokoe's linguistics journal?

6)   What label did Stokoe borrow from Ferguson to describe the variation he saw in ASL?

7)   Why was the Ferguson/Stokoe label inaccurate regarding ASL variation?

8)   What label did James Woodward create to describe the variation he saw in ASL?

9)   Why was Woodward's label inaccurate?

10)   What label did Lucas and Valli suggest as a more accurate identification of the natural variation of ASL that includes some aspects of English?

11)   What grammatical adjustments are necessary for ASL and English to be produced simultaneously?

Section 2 Review Questions

12) What reasons would some deaf people have for refusing to use their speech abilities in public?

13) Why might a DeafBlind person need to be far away from a signer in order to understand them?

14) Who developed manual cues and for what reason were they created?

15) How are consonants and vowels differentiated via manual cues?

16) What is the difference between Computer Assisted Notetaking and Computer Aided Real-time Transcription.

17) Who created the first manual English code?

18) What are the names of each of the three manual English codes mentioned in this Unit?

19) How did manual English codes help bring an end to pure oralism in schools?

20) What language serves as the dominant language of manual English codes?

21) How are manual English codes similar to pidgins?

22) What are the similarities and differences between pidgins and creoles?

American Sign Language and Contact Signing

Battison R. 1978. *Lexical Borrowing in American Sign Language*. Silver Spring, MD: Linstok Press.

Cokely, D., & C. Baker. 1980. *American Sign Language: A Teacher's Resource Text on Grammar and Culture.* Silver Spring, MD: TJ Publishers, Inc.

Klina, E. & U. Bellugi. 1979. *The Signs of Language*. Cambridge, MA: Harvard University Press.

Lucas, Ceil, & Clayton Valli. 1992. *Language Contact in the American Deaf Community*. San Diego, CA: Academic Press.

Maher, J. 1993. William C. Stokoe, Jr. *Deaf Life*, January.

Stokoe, W. 1960. *Sign Language Structure: An Outline of the Visual Communication Systems of the American Deaf.* Burtonsville, MD: Linstok Press.

Stokoe, W. 1965. *The Dictionary of American Sign Language*. Burtonsville, MD: Linstok Press.

Stokoe, William C. 1969. Sign language diglossia. *Studies in Linguistics 21*: 27-41.

Valli, C. & C. Lucas. 1995. *Linguistics of American Sign Language: Revised Edition*. Washington, DC: Gallaudet Press.

Woodward, James C. 1972. Implications for sociolinguistic research among the deaf. *Sign Language Studies 1*: 1-7.

Woodward, James C. 1973. Some characteristics of Pidgin Sign English. *Sign Language Studies 3*: 39-46.

Deafblind & Oral Communication

Haas, Christopher, Earl Fleetwood & Mike Ernest. 1995. An analysis of ASL variation within Deafblind interaction: Question forms, backchanneling, and turn-taking. In *Communication Forum 1995*. L. Byers, J. Chaiken, & M. Mueller, Eds. Washington, DC: Gallaudet University School of Communication.

Kaplan, H, S. Bally, & C. Garretson. 1985. *Speechreading: A Way to Improve Understanding*. Washington, DC: Gallaudet University Press.

Kisor, H. 1990. *What's That Pig Outdoors? A Memoir of Deafness*. New York, NY: Penguin Books.

O'Brien, Stephanie & Candace Steffen. 1996. Tactile ASL: ASL as used by Deafblind persons. In *Communication Forum 1996*. L. Byers & M. Rose, Eds. Washington, DC: Gallaudet University School of Communication.

Sauerburger, D. 1993. *Independence Without Sight or Sound: Suggestions for Practitioners Working with Deaf-Blind Adults*. New York, NY: American Foundation for the Blind.

Smith, T. 1994. *Guidelines: Practical Tips for Working and Socializing with Deaf-Blind People*. Burtonsville, MD: Linstok Press.

Cued Language Transliteration

Cornett, R. O. & M. E. Daisey. 1992. *The Cued Speech Resource Book For Parents of Deaf Children*. Raleigh, NC: National Cued Speech Association.

Crosby, O. 1995. *Silent Dancing: A Journey of Discovery*. Park City, UT: Osmond Crosby.

Fleetwood, E., & M. Metzger. 1990. *Cued Speech Transliteration: Theory and Application*. Silver Spring, MD: Calliope Press.

Fleetwood, E. & M. Metzger. 1998. *Cued Language Structure: An Analysis of Cued American English Based on Linguistic Principles*. Silver Spring, MD: Calliope Press.

Manual Codes and Pidgins

Crabtree, M. & J. Powers, Eds. *Language Files: Materials for an Introduction to Language*. Columbus Ohio: Ohio State University Press.

Crystal, D. 1987. *The Cambridge Encyclopedia of Language*. New York, NY: Cambridge University Press.

Frishberg, N. 1990. *Interpreting: An Introduction*. Silver Spring, MD: RID Press.

Gannon, J. 1981. *Deaf Heritage: A Narrative History of Deaf America*. Silver Spring, MD: National Association of the Deaf.

Lane, H. 1992. *The Mask of Benevolence: Disabling the Deaf Community*. New York: Alfred A. Knopf.

Schwartz, Sue. 1996. Choices in Deafness: A Parent's Guide to Communication Options. Washington, DC: Gallaudet Press.

Supalla, S. 1991. Manually Coded English: The modality question in signed language development. In P. Siple & S. Fischer, (Eds.), *Theoretical Issues in Sign Language Research*. Chicago, IL: The University of Chicago Press.

Deaf Power

> Saturday, March 12. On Saturday hundreds of students and their supporters gathered on campus for a "Board Buster Day." Activities were planned to give everyone a break from the stress of the week. There was a picnic on Hotchkiss Field and free hot dogs and hamburgers were distributed.
>
> The DPN Council continued its twice-a-day meetings, and "Ole Jim" remained full of people and the press awaiting developments.
>
> Members of the board of trustees began returning to Washington for the meeting to pick Gallaudet's eighth president, discuss the remaining student demands, and to finish other business matters that had been postponed because of the protest. ...
>
> Frances M. Rainwood, a supporter from Rockville, Maryland, told the board, "you may have done us a favor... Your action has galvanized us as we haven't been galvanized before." (J. Gannon, 1989: 131-132)

The quick success of the Deaf President Now Protests demonstrated the power of unity. Even as proponents of oral education waited in line behind manual education advocates for a "Board Burger" hamburger or a "Spilman Dog" hotdog, they all shared the knowledge that together they had accomplished much and together they would yet win great victories.

A famous saying states that "Knowledge is Power." Deaf Power began with the founding of residential schools for Deaf children and has solidly depended upon communication, language, and transferring knowledge between its members. This Unit reviews the successes of Deaf people (both as individuals and as groups), the growing number of educational resources for deaf people, and significant technology and events that have advanced the empowerment of deaf people.

Look for the answers to the following questions as you read:

1) How have deaf people demonstrated their human abilities without depending on spoken language?

2) What changes in technology further separated deaf and hearing people in the late 1920's?

3) What organizations have Deaf people founded as a means of serving their own needs?

4) What are the differences between various institutions of higher learning that have programs for deaf students?

5) What legislative acts have had significant impact (good or bad) upon the deaf community?

6) What event set the stage for success during the Deaf President Now protests at Gallaudet University (just one week before the protest)?

7) Who were the key players in the DPN events?

8) What impact has DPN had upon the deaf community?

9) What other major events in the deaf community have spotlighted the talents and abilities of the deaf community?

10) What language phenomenon occurs when deaf people from various countries gather together for several days?

11) What advances have deaf people made in recent years to overcome previous setbacks?

12) What Federal Legislation has improved accessibility of television broadcasts for the deaf community?

13) What Federal Legislation has improved access to interpreting and telecommunication services for deaf people?

14) What is the difference between Deaf culture and the deaf community?

15) What are the key factors involved in core membership in the deaf community?

Section 1 – Deaf Organizations & Socialization
Dummy Hoy & Deaf Athletes

Deaf people played a significant role in the American history of sports. The most accomplished of these was **William E. Hoy** who played fifteen years of major league baseball starting in 1886. Known as "Dummy" Hoy, he invented the hand signals for calling balls (raising the left arm) and strikes (raising the right arm). He also set a record by throwing out three men at home plate from the outfield. Hoy managed to steal 82 bases during his career, which puts him among the top twenty best base-stealing baseball players. William Hoy lived to the age of 99 years and died at the end of 1961. He was not the first, nor the last Deaf person to play professional baseball.

Another Deaf professional baseball player was **Luther** "Dummy" **Taylor** who played for the New York Giants in the early 1900's. During one rainy game, the umpires refused to postpone the game and in the seventh inning, Luther Taylor came to bat wearing rubber galoshes and carrying an umbrella. The resulting laughter was enough to halt the game.

Deaf people are also credited with creating the huddle. The Gallaudet football team began the practice as a way of concealing the discussions of the next play from their competition. Gallaudet also has invented another tactic for the game that is not widely used: rather than depending upon the quarterback to vocally call out the commands for movement on the field, a huge drum is used from the sidelines. During the huddle the Gallaudet team will agree on which beat of the drum they will all move. Once in position, the drummer starts slowly beating the drum, usually between one and three times, depending on whether the team moves after each beat. The Gallaudet team has a history of using this drum to their advantage. First they begin by consistently moving on the second beat of the drum, until the other team is conditioned to it. Then they will set up a play on which the team does not move until the third beat. Almost every time it is tried the other team will have a player or two who moves on the second beat, thus causing a penalty and the Gallaudet team gains a few yards.

Another claim to fame are the world records set by **Kitty O'Neil**, a professional stunt woman and hollywood actor. Kitty, an orally-educated deaf woman, broke the world record for speed in women's water-skiing in 1970. She also broke several of the woman's land speed records for a rocket car in 1976 and in 1977.

Sporting events are generally very popular among deaf people. The simplest explanation for the popularity of sports is that they are visually accessible events and do not need to be interpreted. With hand signals used to indicate time outs and penalty calls in football, baseball, basketball, hockey, volleyball, and so on, little explanation is needed once the deaf spectator understands the rules of the game. Additionally, deaf people tend to be on a more equal footing with their hearing peers when participating in sports activities since their ability to play the game dominates over the ability to hear and speak.

The American Athletic Association for the Deaf was founded by deaf people in Akron, Ohio in 1945. The AAAD provides organizational structure and a hall of fame for a variety of sports associations serving deaf people. The AAAD organizes the American competitors who participate in the World Games for the Deaf - otherwise known as the Deaf Olympics.

In recent times deaf people have been chosen to play on USA Olympic teams and even the television show "American Gladiators" (both as a gladiator and as contestants).

In addition to these opportunities there are deaf sporting events from local deaf club teams to the teams at residential schools.

Deaf Actors & Silent Films

During the silent film era it didn't matter what your voice sounded like if you were a film actor. Some of the best known actors and actresses of that era had their careers ruined when soundtracks became a standard feature of movies after *The Jazz Singer* was premiered on October 6th, 1927. These hearing actors just didn't have voices that matched their screen personalities.

The silent film era provided wonderful entertainment to deaf and hearing audience members alike. Since there was no soundtrack, all of the dialogue was accessible through written English. Many of the actors on screen were Deaf too, some of them even popular in their time. The most widely recognized Deaf actor in the 1920's was **Granville Redmond** who played a dance-hall manager in Charlie Chaplin's film *A Dog's Life*, and many other roles as well. Usually the roles played by deaf actors were not deaf characters. This would be reversed for several decades after the 1920's.

Once the silent era had faded completely, hearing actors would be employed to portray deaf characters. One of the most famous roles was that of *Johnny Belinda* in 1948. This role of a deaf girl as the main character of the story won an Oscar for the hearing actress who portrayed her: Jane Wyman. While this character was one of the first to use American Sign Language in a film seen mostly by hearing people, the Deaf community would comment that it was clearly a hearing person's signing. Hollywood would repeat this offense to deaf people many times over the next several decades as hearing actors who had no connection with the deaf community would be hired to play culturally Deaf roles.

One of the breakthroughs for Deaf actors was Mark Medoff's play *Children of a Lesser God*. This play portrays the conflict between the deaf and hearing worlds and provides a lead role (Sarah Norman) designed specifically for a Deaf actress. **Phyllis Frelich** originated that role and became the first deaf person to win a Tony award for "Best Actress". In fact, Mark Medoff had written the play specifically for Phyllis Frelich to have a lead role in a play which used ASL and English throughout. **Marlee Matlin** would repeat the performance of Sarah Norman in the 1986 film version and became the first Deaf person to earn an Oscar award for Best Actress in 1987. Even with this recognition, Hollywood still did not acknowledge the need to have Deaf actors portray Deaf characters.

In 1992, Penny Marshall was the executive producer for a film called *Calendar Girl*. The film called for a minor character who was deaf and used signed language. Although deaf actors auditioned for the part, none were chosen and the role was assigned to a hearing actor who knew no signed language. The Deaf community decided to take action. A nation-wide protest was arranged through the National Association of the Deaf. The film's release date was postponed but eventually the film opened to poor reviews and protests in major cities in the U.S. The film never performed well and the Deaf community saw the results as verification that their protest efforts had been productive.

Deaf characters on television have also generally been portrayed by hearing people, as recently as 1997 when the movie *Breaking Through* cast a hearing actress in the role of an abused deaf girl. One of the earliest breakthroughs for deaf actors came in 1967 when the *NBC Special: Experiment in Television* showcased the National Theatre of the Deaf, which had just that year been established in Waterford, Connecticut at the Eugene O'Neil Theatre Center. NTD members appeared on national television six years later in the *A Child's Christmas in Wales.* In 1985 NBC aired the Hallmark Hall of Fame: *Love is Never Silent* in which all the deaf characters are portrayed by deaf actors (many of whom had been previously associated with the National Theatre of the Deaf).

Entertainment By, And For, The Deaf Community

One of the most traditional forms of entertainment in the Deaf community has been story-telling. No particular technology is required but excellent mastery of signed language will make a significant impression upon the audience. Before movies and television became commonplace the deaf community regularly convened at deaf clubs across the United States and would attend dramatic signed performances of literature, poetry, and plays.

When silent movies became common, deaf people enjoyed equal access to the acting and dialogue of popular films. Upon the widespread use of soundtracks, however, deaf people were left guessing the plots and dialogue of every film. Three Deaf men worked to create films for deaf audiences.

Charles Kraul and **Charles Yanzito** used their movie camera to document the activities of the Deaf community, primarily through the Fraternal Society of the Deaf which would have national conventions in different cities around the country. The Fraternal Society of the Deaf was an organization created in 1901 to provide life insurance to Deaf people. The Frat (as it is popularly known) had national conventions every four years.

Ernest Marshall used his own movie equipment to make narrative films, sometimes translations of famous authors, but usually based on his own screenplays. These films would be shown at deaf clubs around the country. Marshall actually required that he personally travel to the deaf clubs partly to ensure the safety of his films, but mostly to provide the opportunity to meet other deaf people across the country.

When television became widely popular in the 1950's there were more opportunities for deaf people to find visual entertainment. **Bernard Bragg** had moved from New York to San Francisco to follow his teaching career. He had acted in plays and benefits for the deaf community for years and found himself doing short mime skits on the local television in San Francisco. From 1958 until 1961 he performed his own "The Quiet Man" show on KQED and also performed in local nightclubs. Bragg met Marcel Marceau and ended up being invited to study mime in Paris. Eventually he became a co-founder of the **National Theatre of the Deaf**, originally based in Waterford, Connecticut. He performed in NBC's 1967 *Experiment in TV,* which created controversy for oralists by showing deaf people using signed language on national television. In 1973, Bragg served as an exchange artist in Moscow's Theatre of Mimicry and Gesture.

The National Theatre of the Deaf had a majority of Deaf actors, but its board had only a solitary token deaf person and the Deaf community often complained that the theatre was of the deaf, but not for the deaf. The plays were only rarely creations of deaf playwrights, most of the repertoire being traditional plays performed in contact ASL which made it difficult for Deaf audiences to fully enjoy the performances. Hearing people made up the majority of the audiences.

In 1974 Gil Eastman wrote a play *Sign Me Alice*, which adapted the *My Fair Lady* theme of transforming someone's common, everyday language to a "higher" form. In this case, however, the transformation is from Alice's native ASL to the artificial pidgin of manual English code. Instead of falling in love with her educator, Alice decides to return to her roots and rejects the teachings and philosophy of the manual English code proponents.

NTD relocated to Chester, Connecticut in 1983 and then in 2000 moved again to Hartford, Connecticut – the historic home city of the American School for the Deaf where Deaf education got its start in North America. Dozens of Deaf theatre companies now exist world-wide, many of them founded by NTD alumni.

In 1980 Bernard Bragg and **Eugene Bergman** co-wrote a play entitled *Tales from a Clubroom*, which was first performed at the centennial NAD convention in 1980.[16] Deaf audiences finally connected with a play written by, for, and about deaf people. The play would be reprised in 1989 at the Deaf Way Conference to much acclaim from deaf audiences. Bragg concluded, however, that while deaf audiences enjoyed the play, there was good reason for most of the efforts of the NTD to be directed toward hearing audiences:

> The sad truth that sank into me is that deaf audiences are simply too small, the deaf being too small a minority, to sustain a thriving deaf professional theater. To survive, plays about the deaf must be geared to hearing audiences by focusing on universal experiences and conflicts between the hearing and the deaf worlds. This accounts for the success of such plays as Mark Medoff's *Children of a Lesser God*. (Bragg, 1989: p 193)

Although the material performed may not be related exclusively to the deaf community, we now see that the performances of the NTD, and many other local deaf theatre groups which have since emerged, is that they now perform in much more natural ASL, and have therefore become much more accessible and entertaining to deaf audiences.

The NTD did provide nurturing for a few Deaf playwrights, directors, and actors. **Shanny Mow** was the first Deaf playwright to have NTD stage an original Deaf play - an adaptation of the Trojan War entitled *The Iliad, Play by Play*. **Edmund Waterstreet** directed the play and became the first Deaf director of an NTD production written by a deaf playwright. In 1975 Shanny Mow established the world's first resident professional signed language theater - the Fairmount Theatre of the Deaf[17] - in Cleveland. Waterstreet has had numerous nationally-broadcast television roles from *Love is Never Silent* to *Reasonable Doubts*.

Other early members of the NTD include **Linda Bove,** who performed on *Days of Our Lives* and *Sesame Street*; **Patrick Graybill,** who became a professor of theatre and an educational film maker; and Gil Eastman who chaired Gallaudet's Theatre department, hosted the Emmy-winning *Deaf Mosaic* news program, and wrote the book *A Deaf Person's Thoughts*.

---

[16] Bergman and Bragg would eventually publish the play in 1981.
[17] They later changed their name to the Cleveland Signstage Theatre.

Another group of actors in Northern California called themselves D.E.A.F. Media and put together a five-year Emmy-winning series of television programs called *Silent Perspectives* which ran on the local PBS channel in San Mateo, California from 1974 until 1979. *Silent Perspectives* was an interview/talk show designed for the Deaf community. In 1979 they produced a second project called *Rainbows End*, which was essentially a Deaf *Sesame Street*. Five episodes of *Rainbows End* were funded by a Federal Grant, but no additional shows were put together. Several of the members of D.E.A.F. Media have continued and broadened their acting careers: **Ella Mae Lentz** is one of the co-authors who put together the *Signing Naturally* ASL textbooks and videotapes. **Freda Norman**, who was also a member of the NTD, has been involved in some of the Signing Naturally videotapes as well as numerous video projects involving ASL storytelling. **Howie Seago** joined the NTD and later portrayed Deaf characters in various television shows including a *Star Trek - The Next Generation* episode.

The National Fraternal Society of the Deaf

The origins of the National Fraternal Society of the Deaf are found in an 1898 alumni reunion for graduates of the Michigan School for the Deaf in Flint Michigan. Thirteen graduates gathered to discuss the difficulties they experienced in buying life insurance. The insurance industry at that time believed (incorrectly) that deaf people were prone to accidents and therefore had shorter-than-average life expectancies. The graduates assigned various responsibilities to investigate the possibilities and within three years they established what was then called the Fraternal Society of the Deaf with **Peter Hellers** of Detroit as the Grand President.

Life insurance was the first kind of insurance that the group provided. The original means of insurance was that members would each contribute an equal amount upon the death of another member. The first claim for benefits required each member to contribute $1.00 to cover the funeral costs of Chicago member George Tate who had died at the age of 26. Expanded life insurance benefits, sickness insurance, and accident insurance were added over the years.

Originally run out of the homes of the officers, the organization rented office space in 1905 in Chicago. Two years later the organization was incorporated in the state of Illinois as the National Fraternal Society of the Deaf. Membership and assets grew as the organization began serving a social function by hosting a national convention every four years in various large cities around the country. Local divisions in over 100 locations in the United States and Canada also provide support and long-term commitment to the organization.

Strong leadership from its officers, all of whom were deaf, allowed the organization to survive the great depression. Having invested largely in mortgages, the first home office owned by the organization was actually obtained through a foreclosure. Offices have been relocated several more times and are now at 1118 South Sixth Street, Springfield, IL. Through the example of the NFSD, (known in the Deaf community simply as "The Frat") national insurance companies learned that deaf people were no greater an insurance risk than anyone else. Although this has resulted in greater competition from other insurance companies, the Frat has continued to increase its assets and its ability to serve its members. By the year 2001, the Society was licensed to do business in 36 states.

Once automobile ownership became common place, deaf drivers found that they were being charged higher rates for automobile insurance. The NFSD became involved in advocating for fair insurance rates for deaf drivers in the 1940s. Over the years various states attempted to pass legislation against deaf drivers and the NFSD was largely successful in their efforts to defeat such legislation. Deaf drivers now find themselves able to obtain automobile insurance at the same rates as hearing drivers.

Aside from the local chapters and national conventions, the NSFD also provides a national news link through its magazine The Frat. The organization also provides scholarships to deaf students across the country. The local chapters, too, have a tradition of providing scholarships, awards, and service projects for their communities.

CSUN, NTID & the Expansion of Post-Secondary Eductation Options for Deaf Students

Back in the 1960s there was a general increase in the post-secondary education options of deaf people. Prior to this time deaf people could only obtain a visually accessible College education through Gallaudet College. Many deaf people did obtain degrees through other colleges but did so without interpreting services. California and Illinois started the trend in 1960 by providing programs to serve the needs of deaf students in college courses. By the end of the decade there would be thirteen alternatives to Gallaudet for deaf students all around the country, although most of them did not have any deaf faculty members. Today Federal Law requires every school to provide accommodations for deaf students, but some schools still provide programs designed specifically for recruiting deaf students.

In 1964 the California State University at Northridge (CSUN) began a program to address the needs of deaf students. The program quickly grew into a coordinated set of services for Deaf students attending the school, including interpreting services. Some of the faculty members at CSUN are deaf. Courses that relate to the deaf community (sign language, deaf education, interpreter training) are taught in ASL. Deaf students can access all other courses offered at the school through organized interpreting services. CSUN serves the largest number of deaf students West of the Mississippi river.

In 1968 the Federal Government established the second college specifically for deaf people when the National Technical Institute for the Deaf was established as a school within the Rochester Institute of Technology in Rochester, NY. This school was established to provide a technical school alternative to Gallaudet College. Many faculty members at NTID are deaf. A wide variety of courses are taught in ASL. Students can earn many Associate Degrees at NTID without taking any classes through interpreting services. Deaf students are also able to pursue any level of education from undergraduate to post-graduate through centralized interpreting services that allow them to take courses at any of the other schools of RIT.

Section 2 – Deaf Activism & Legislation
Section 504 and PL 94-142

Two laws in the 1970s provided Federal legislation on behalf of disabled Americans. These laws affect the Deaf community as well. Section 504 of the Rehabilitation Act of 1973 requires all organizations receiving federal funds to make their programs accessible to disabled people. Public Law 94-142 opened the doors of public education to all children with disabilities.

Section 504 of the Rehabilitation Act of 1973

Section 504 of the Rehabilitation Act of 1973 is enforced by the Office of Civil Rights (OCR) under the guidelines of the Department of Education. Section 504 protects the civil and constitutional rights of people with disabilities. It prohibits organizations that receive federal funds from discriminating against otherwise qualified individuals on the sole basis of a mental or physical disability. Section 504 applies to public education through any college or university that accepts federal funding. Other institutions that are affected are all federal government agencies, most state-level agencies and hospitals. For Deaf and DeafBlind people the law provides a mechanism to obtain access to information through interpreters, but this right to access must be asserted by the consumer and is not outlined in great detail in the legislation. The Americans with Disabilities Act (1990) applied the same basic concepts of Section 504 to the private (non-government) sector and also provided much more specific definitions and requirements.

The Education of All Handicapped Children Act (PL 94-142)

While Section 504 is widely regarded as having been a strongly positive contribution to the Deaf community, PL 94-142 has not received such high regard. Although the law opened the doors to public education, residential schools for deaf children have been weakened through lower enrollment. Research (J. Cerney, 2004) has indicated that there are significant negative effects on self-esteem and personal motivation when Deaf children are placed outside of their own "mainstream" (deaf peers and ASL-fluent teachers and role models). While U.S. legislation identifies the best educational placement as the "Least Restrictive Environment", the Canadian legislation uses the terms "Most Enabling".

The Individuals with Disabilities Education Act, a federal law, was passed and signed by president Gerald Ford in 1975. It was reauthorized in 1990 and comes up for regular review in the United States congress. The law mandates that all children receive a free, appropriate public education regardless of the level or severity of their disability. Children ages 3 through 21 who need special education services because of a disabling condition are eligible. Funding is provided to assist states in their education of students with disabilities. States must ensure that students receive an individualized education program based on their needs in the "least restrictive environment". P.L. 94-142 assumes that the "Least Restrictive Environment" is NOT a segregated school setting and that "unless a child's individualized education program requires some other arrangement, the child is (to be) educated in the school which he or she would attend if not disabled [Section 121a.522(c)]." The law states that removing a child from the regular classroom should only happen when the child's educational needs "with the use of supplementary aids and services cannot be achieved satisfactorily [Section 121a.550(2)]."

P.L. 94-142 provides guidelines for determining which services are necessary and provides "due process" to ensure that these needs are met. One of the guidelines is the use of IEPs. The term "IEP" refers to the **Individualized Education Program** (or Plan). This is a written, legal document that identifies the special education and support services that will be provided to the student. The IEP team members decide what services will be provided and what the goals will be to determine successful results. Team members should include representatives from each of the following groups: administration, teachers, special education service coordinators, and parents/guardians of the children. Older children (middle school and above) should participate in their own IEP meetings. P.L. 94-142 asserts that parents are permitted to inspect and review the records of their children in a timely manner. If parents are not satisfied with any part of the IEP then they can refuse to sign the IEP and make use of due process options guaranteed by the law. An IEP meeting may still occur without a parent attending if the parent is unable or unwilling to attend. Generally an IEP may be "re-opened" at any time by parent request. P.L. 94-142 requires that the following items be included in an IEP:
  * the student's present educational performance levels;
  * the yearly goals and the instructional objectives;
  * the special education services;
  * the dates that service begins and how long it will last;
  * transition services for each student age 14 and older;

Gallaudet University and the "Deaf President Now!" Revolution

On April 8th, 1864, Abraham Lincoln signed the bill that created the National Deaf Mute College. Its first president was the son of Thomas Hopkins Gallaudet and Sophia Fowler: Edward Miner Gallaudet, or EMG. EMG was born into a signing family with a deaf mother. Thus the first president of what became Gallaudet University was a native user of American Sign Language, but was not deaf. Subsequent presidents were all hearing, none were native signers, and several didn't know any signs when they applied for the job.

In 1969, Edward C. Merrill became president and was the first person to head the school who had not come to the position through teaching deaf people. Merrill had been the dean of the College of Education at the University of Tennessee. During his tenure, Merrill increased the number of deaf administrators and was working to provide the opportunity for deaf people to replace him upon his retirement in 1983. The next president was not deaf, and again, was not from within Gallaudet's administration. His name was Lloyd Johns and had been an administrator at the University of California at Sacramento. He remained as president only a few months, however, and resigned in 1983. Rather than open up the search process again (or offer the job to the second-runner up) the Board of Trustees chose to elevate the vice president of business affairs, Jerry C. Lee, to the position of president of Gallaudet. This was announced as a temporary solution, but within a year he became the final and official choice of the board of trustees for president. The Gallaudet faculty were not pleased because Lee had not risen through the ranks of an academic faculty: he had served only as an administrator.

When Jerry C. Lee announced his intention to retire in December of 1987, many people saw it as the opportunity to finally have a deaf person as president, but most of this movement was among deaf faculty members, rather than the students. In January of

1988 there was no president of the University. Lee had retired in December and a committee of four hearing administrators was carrying out the administrative duties of the president's office. The Board of Trustees, with a minority of four deaf members, was under the direction of Jane Bassett Spilman. There was already a perception that things were not being done ethically because Jerry C. Lee had retired from Gallaudet in order to accept a vice-presidency with the Bassett furniture company, under the direction of Jane Bassett Spilman's husband. By February, 1988, the board had reduced the total number of candidates for the presidency to six quarter-finalists, three of them were deaf.

In February a flyer went out to the students and faculty:

> It's time! In 1842, a Roman Catholic became president of the University of Notre Dame. In 1875, a woman became president of Wellesley College. In 1886, a Jew became president of Yeshiva University. In 1926, a Black person became president of Howard University.
>
> AND in 1988, the Gallaudet University presidency belongs to a DEAF person. To show OUR solidarity behind OUR mandate for a deaf president of OUR University, you are invited to participate in a historic RALLY!

Many faculty members did not officially cancel classes. Some were sympathetic to the cause of having a deaf president for cultural reasons, others were against the idea of advocating that hearing status be the primary factor in determining an administrator. The majority of students did not have any particular preference for whether the president was deaf or not. To them the president was only the person that they saw on the Gallaudet cable televisions with his monthly presentation to the University or at graduation ceremonies. The president of Gallaudet University was not significant to them and many were not aware that there had never been a deaf president before. Some students even thought that a new president had already been selected and had been in charge since January.

The Rally was organized by a few graduates of Gallaudet, mostly people who worked in the metropolitan business community around Gallaudet. They set up an event which would do more than just present a pep rally, but rather an education for the reasons why Gallaudet needed a deaf president. At the beginning of the rally there were between 500 to 1,000 people at the football field. Here we learned about the overall need for a deaf president from a historical perspective. From there we moved to the Kendall Demonstration Elementary School and learned about the importance from a social and developmental perspective as a role model for primary and secondary students. We continued our journey to the Hall Memorial Building, the main building of classrooms and faculty offices, and learned about the need for a deaf person administrating a school for deaf people. The next step was outside the President's residence where we learned that the building which was the most prominent living quarters on a campus full of deaf people had no visual door or phone signalers, no tty, no captioning because it had never had a deaf resident. Finally we gathered at the statue of Edward Miner Gallaudet, the first president, the one who was a native signer, and we were reminded of the national and international implications of having a deaf president and what it meant to the deaf people of the United States and of the world symbolically. By this time there were over 2,000 people taking this educational tour of the Gallaudet campus and they had become well convinced of the need for a deaf president.

Almost one week later, on Sunday, March 6th, 1988, hundreds of people gathered outside the main gymnasium expecting to enter and find a seat in time for the announcement of the Board's decision. The gym was locked and so the growing crowd waited outside. At about an hour before the expected announcement time, a stack of pre-printed announcements[18] was delivered to the waiting crowd, announcing that Elisabeth Ann Zinser had been selected from among the three finalists. She was the only hearing person out of the three and although she had the most impressive resume of the finalists, she had the least knowledge of the deaf community, of American Sign Language, or of the education of deaf people at any level. The crowd was visibly disappointed, but not yet moved to action. And they remained.

The crowd grew larger as more people came to see the announcement in the gym only to learn that there would be no announcement, no people to complain to, only a sheet of paper to explain the Board's decision. Soon there was discussion of protesting. The crowd moved out into Florida Avenue in front of the University. The police directed traffic around the growing crowd who sat and watched Gary Olsen from the National Association of the Deaf, and Jerry Covell, a student activist, lay out a plan of peaceful resistance. Olsen stressed that if any of us were arrested, the rest must not be scared away but stay seated in the street and wait for the police to carry them away. Do not fight, but do not run. We were angry with the Board of Trustees, not with the police, and we would let our protest speak our disappointment in their decision.

No one was arrested. The police continued to direct traffic around us and we continued to lay out a plan of action. Someone pointed out that the Board of Trustees were still meeting at the Mayflower Hotel, downtown. Soon it was decided that we would walk to the Mayflower hotel and take our protest to the Board members. So our group of between five hundred and one-thousand people began to walk Northwest on Florida Avenue toward the police that had been directing traffic around us. We had not told them what we were planning to do. As more of their vehicles moved to block our path, we began to run toward them and around their now helpless vehicles (never try to stop a group of people on foot by putting a car in their way!) We kept up the pace at a fast jog until we were under the railroad bridge and at the intersection with New York Avenue. Here a few people (who would later be given the responsibilities of student leaders) told us to stop and wait for the others because we were stringing our group out too far. Once we had regrouped well enough, we walked Southwest down New York Avenue chanting "Deaf President Now! Deaf President Now!"

1988 was an election year. George Bush would end up running against Michael Dukakis in August but in March, the field was wide open as Pat Robertson and Bob Dole challenged Bush for the Republican Nomination. Jesse Jackson was challenging Mike Dukakis and several other contenders for the Democratic Nomination. To the citizens of Washington, DC, a crowd of people walking down New York Avenue after 8:00 pm on a Sunday evening, chanting "Deaf President Now!" must have been a curious sight. Even with Gallaudet in their backyard, many were unaware of the fact that Washington, DC had a college specifically for deaf people.

When we arrived at the Mayflower hotel (after one student had asked directions of a police officer how to get there... he told us!) we took over the street in front of the

---

[18] Announcements had also been pre-printed to announce each of the other two finalists.

building. Police cars were all around and soon there was a local television station's roving camera van parked across the street. We sat outside and chanted "Deaf President Now!" and held more discussions about our plans of action. We demanded to have Jane Bassett Spilman come down and tell us why the Board had voted to select a hearing person for the presidency. Some representatives were selected to go up to the Board and meet with them to determine the motivation and to express our disappointment. The rest of us waited. We laid out a deadline that we would wait until 10:30 for Ms. Spilman to speak with us. If she did not come, we would leave... first to the White House and then to the Capitol.

At 10:30, Spilman had not come and soon afterward we split up with most of us heading to the White House (with Ronald Reagan inside) and the rest staying behind to keep the pressure on the Board. Jane Bassett Spilman eventually spoke to this smaller crowd, offering no more explanation than that the board of trustees had met its legal obligation to select the best person and they had done their job fairly, in the open, and with input from faculty, staff, and students who had all provided favorable comments regarding Dr. Zinser. The main body of the crowd had already arrived at the White House and within a minute, there was a person standing every thirty feet or so on the other side of the fence that surrounds the White House. We were instructed not to climb on the fence, but otherwise we could remain as long as we were peaceful. We stayed a short time. A news camera took some footage. Then we headed toward the Capitol building and then the crowd headed back to Gallaudet's Hugh's Gymnasium for a planning session. Those who headed for home had instructions to return to the main gates of the campus at 5:00 am the next morning.

With only a few hours of sleep, we returned to the main gates. Already there were a number of cars parked blocking the main entrance from vehicular access. Many deaf employees attempted to enter and upon discovering the Board's decision the previous night, parked their cars near the campus and joined the ever-growing crowd at the main gate. Eventually the cars were removed (with the threat of being towed) for emergency access reasons. But the crowd remained and allowed access only to news media and a few other vehicles. The campus was declared closed by the Provost and there were discussions and presentations to the crowd discussion further action. Rumors were milling about that Nightline would do a special show on the protest but we were not the topic that night. We did, however, make the national news broadcasts that night.

Tuesday the campus was open, although no classes were attended. It was pay day and also the week before Spring break so it seemed that economics had determined the course of action that day. The students had organized and selected a group of four leaders. One was the past president of the Student Body Government, **Tim Rarus**. Another was the newly installed president, **Greg Hlibok** (Greg's first day as SBG president had been March 1st, the day of the Rally). **Jerry Covell** was chosen, as was **Bridgetta Bourne**, who had been involved in the SBG as well. All were from deaf families, and all were (or would become) government majors.

Wednesday saw the campus closed down again and more media coverage. By now the media was learning how to deal with interpreting services for interviews (they had always tried to put the camera on the interpreter or put the interpreter next to the deaf person signing). The students were learning that the television cameras would roll more often when they became noisy crowds chanting with their voices, rather than silently. With their deaf voices, thousands chanted "Deaf President Now!" before the cameras.

Reporters looked for people wearing armbands[19] of various colours which identified them as student leaders, student support leaders, or interpreters. The Faculty senate gathered for a special session and so did the Gallaudet staff members. Both bodies voted to support the students' demand for a deaf president. Greg Hlibok and Dr. Zinser were both on Nightline that evening.[20]

Thursday included more encouragement to hang on. People were being encouraged to give up Spring break and continue the protest. Some feared that the protest would end when students left for break. Many had non-refundable airline tickets. That evening, Dr. Zinser concluded that she was being perceived as the person preventing progress and she resigned at 7:30 pm that evening. The news spread later that evening and people rejoiced; but the protest continued.

On Friday Greg Hlibok wore a button, which said "3 & 1/2." It represented the fact that of the four demands,[21] only the first half of the first demand had been accomplished. We still did not yet have a deaf president. That afternoon we marched on the Capitol and the White House. This was the third march on the Capitol building in six days and was the first to actually have been awarded a permit. Permits for demonstrations generally require two weeks notice... this one had been achieved in only a few days. Chances were that we would have marched without a permit anyway... excitement was very high on

---

[19] Soon many groups would identify themselves with armbands including the Gallaudet Dance Company who was scheduled for a tour over spring break. There was pressure from the protesters to cancel the trip because it would give the impression that Gallaudet was open and the protests were having no effect. The dance company members used armbands as part of their solution because they would wear them as a symbol of support and tell every audiences about the struggle for a deaf president.

[20] Marlee Matlin was a third guest. She was chosen to appear simply because of her fame as an actress and therefore she was the most well-known Deaf person in Nightline's audience. She had not previously taken any role in the protests. During the televised discussion, Zinser tried to shift the subject to Matlin by asking how Matlin had dealt with her own difficulty with protesting students. Matlin appeared to not know what Zinser was talking about and may honestly not have known. Zinser was talking about the controversy surrounding Matlin's 1987 award of an honorary doctoral degree during Gallaudet's graduation ceremonies (Matlin had just won the Oscar Award for Best Actress in the Spring of 1987). During the week leading to Matlin's acceptance of the honorary degree, many students were organizing a protest based on the argument that she had not yet earned even an Associates degree. Some students had planned to throw eggs during the ceremony. Seating was reassigned, students were required to carry their gowns to the academic building and dress there (so as not to tape eggs to their arms under their gowns) and Board members personally introduced themselves to known protest leaders (a way of saying "we know who you are.") The honorary degree was awarded without the slightest disturbance, although there were several rows of nervous graduate students sitting in the front rows prepared to duck at a moment's notice. Matlin reportedly was never informed about these events prior to receiving her honorary degree and would only have later found out through the "grapevine."

[21] The four demands had been established originally by the President's Council on Deafness, an advisory board to Gallaudet's President. Once the DPN Council was established, one of its first acts was to officially adopt these four demands:

1) That Dr. Zinser resign and a deaf person be selected as president of Gallaudet University
2) That Jane Bassett Spilman resign as chair of the Board of Trustees
3) That the Board of Trustees be reconstituted to contain a majority of deaf people
4) That no reprisals be taken against participants in the protest

Friday since Zinser had announced her resignation and hundreds of people were arriving at Gallaudet from all across the United States to lend their physical support to the movement. Money was being raised very quickly with the American Postal Workers Union contributing significantly. Again we made the evening national news broadcasts and Greg Hlibok was chosen as ABC's "Person of the Week."

Saturday was a peaceful party at Gallaudet. With the resignation of Zinser we knew it was a only a matter of time until the board chose one of the other two finalists (both of whom were deaf) to replace her as President. The message was that even if a Deaf president was selected, the other three demands had to be met before the protests would end. The focus of these were on the Board of trustees. The menu for the day's picnic reflected this as "Spilman dogs" and "Board Burgers" were served to everyone for for free. The sun was shining with a light breeze, kites were flown, and an air of celebration filled the campus. We were prepared to continue the fight until all the demands were met.

On Sunday afternoon, March 13, 1988, the Board met again. Spilman not only resigned as chair of the Board but resigned from the Board entirely; Phil Bravin, a deaf board member and the chair of the presidential search committee, was chosen to replace her; I. King Jordan was selected as the next president; and steps were taken to increase the numbers of deaf people on the board. Before this was announced to the public, Phil Bravin called Greg Hlibok at Gallaudet's campus. Greg had to be found and then called to the Alumni Association office (this office had served as headquarters to the movement). Phil asked Greg what his brothers' names were in order to confirm that it really was Greg on the other end of the TTY call[22]. As the call progressed, Greg announced the pieces of news that were conveyed to the growing crowd. Phil asked if Greg could guarantee that the campus would be open the next morning (Monday) for business as usual. Greg agreed and the celebrations began. In only one week, the DPN protests had succeeded.

In May of that year the senior class of Gallaudet became the first ever to receive their degrees from a Deaf president. If there had been any doubt of the impact of having a deaf president on the students it was obvious by comparing the graduation ceremonies of 1987 and 1988. In 1988 the President was hugged by half the graduating seniors... in 1987 no one had even considered doing such a thing. The spirit of freedom and self-empowerment had settled permanently into Gallaudet and there was a renewed pride in graduation ceremonies from that time forward.

---

[22] Since TTY communication is text-based, it is not possible to "recognize" someone's voice on a TTY call, although it is possible to recognize a typing style if you are familiar with the person's tendencies on TTY calls.

The "Deaf Way" Conferences

During the week of July 9 - 14, 1989 more than 6,000 people from all over the world came to Washington, DC for the largest gathering of deaf people in history. To understand the impact of that many deaf people, consider that the numbers of deaf people at the Deaf Way were greater than the entire deaf population of the United States when the NAD had been founded in 1880. At every event the majority of people were using signed languages to communicate and there was a spirit of joy as deaf people from eighty-one different countries gathered to learn and be entertained. The two years of planning began while Jerry C. Lee was still president of Gallaudet. The Deaf President Now movement came and went while plans were still in progress for this gathering, and as usual with successful deaf events, it had been planned and executed by deaf people themselves.

Hundreds of people worked behind the scenes and hundreds more on stages, in lecture rooms and in exhibit spaces. There were *thirty-seven poster discussions, seventy-five films or video shows, one thousand visual arts performers*, and *five hundred lectures* packed into *six days*. Events took place simultaneously at the Omni Shorham hotel in Northwest Washington, DC and the Gallaudet Campus in Northeast DC. Shuttle buses provided transportation between the two locations throughout the day and evening. Three hundred and fifty people provided interpreting and translation services. The opening performance was so large that the Lisner auditorium on George Washington University's campus could not hold them all and so it was broadcast by satellite to Gallaudet's campus (thirty blocks away) for an overflow crowd.

Financial support was provided by AT&T and Ronald McDonald Children's Charities with additional support from Coca Cola, the National Endowment for the Arts and from Gallaudet University. An international Deaf Club was established under a tent near the football field. Although performances occurred constantly under the tent, the most interesting thing to see was the evolution of a temporary pidgin language being created from the signed languages of the world. Starting with ASL and Gestuno, the mix of languages and personal styles developed daily into its own variation of what has come to be known as International Signs. This same phenomenon happens at every international gathering of deaf people but the result is always colored by the mix of languages in the environment. Communication flowed well at the event not in spite of deafness but because of it. Deaf people around the world are used to working out communication with other people and when they gather in large groups, their lifetime communication training kicks into high gear and language barriers disappear. As one participant said: If ever there will be world peace, it will start with the international Deaf community!

The Deaf Way conference showcased the abilities of deaf people and was truly an intensive cultural event. It has yet to be duplicated as far as numbers of attendees or the numbers of exhibits, presentations, or artistic performances. This was the World's Fair of the international deaf community. The Deaf Way conference has inspired a number of smaller scale conferences and festivals celebrating the deaf community. Some of these events occur annually.

Deaf Way II was held in July of 2002. It coincided with the National Association of the Deaf's biennial convention and with an international interpreting symposium. Nearly ten thousand people attended and participated in Deaf Way II.

Closed Captioning and Assistive Devices

In 1964, Robert Weitbrecht, a deaf man, invented the acoustic coupler. This simple device by itself was no major advancement for communication technology but serving as a link between existing phone lines and existing teletype equipment, the acoustic coupler became the single most important technological advancement for deaf people in the 1960's. Deaf people were finally able to use the telephone for direct communication without depending on interpreters.

Assistive devices are not limited to the Deaf community. Hearing people use assistive devices all the time: telephones, radios, televisions, alarm clocks, smoke detectors, and door bells. None of these devices are essential for living, but they have become accepted as standard advantages of living in the modern age. Assistive devices for deaf people are simply parallel opportunities for deaf people to enjoy the advantages of the modern age. Even the devices designed specifically for deaf people have benefits for other people. Closed captioning is one clear example because it has been cited as a tool for teaching written English to children and to people learning English as a second language. Vibration pads under the pillow and attached to an alarm clock can help awaken the heavy sleeper who always sleeps through the alarm.

In 1971 television became more accessible when the Caption Center at WBGH in Boston began running open captions on broadcasts of Julia Child's "The French Chef." For the first time in the history of television deaf people had access to the spoken communication of a popular television show. Two years later (in 1973) agreements were made between ABC and PBS for the ABC Evening News to be rebroadcast with open captions on PBS. For six years the Captioned ABC Evening News was the only national news broadcast accessible to the deaf community and the deaf community was regularly tuning in.

Complaints about open captioning were being received from hearing viewers and efforts were made to develop a caption encoding system that would allow captions to be broadcast with regular television signals and then decoded the captions in the viewer's home. "Line-21 closed captioning" was developed by the Caption Center staff with support from ABC. In 1979, the federal government helped establish the National Captioning Institute to expand captioning and to manufacture and distribute closed caption decoders. On March 16, 1980, the first television shows were broadcast with closed captions. A total of 16 hours of closed captioning were offered that spring. For years, ABC was the closed caption leader including the Sunday night movie and much of its prime time lineup.

Over the years captioning technology improved and real time captioning was used to provide captioning of all three major network news broadcasts and all network prime time shows. More and more films have been captioned which make them accessible both on cable and through home video rentals and sales. The cost of close caption decoders has also decreased over the years so that more and more people have been able to access more and more captioning services every year since 1980.

The ADA – Americans with Disabilities Act

The year 1990 saw the passage of two landmark laws for deaf people: on July 26th, the Americans with Disabilities Act (ADA) was signed into law by President George H.W. Bush. Several months later the Television Decoder Circuitry Act was also signed into law. While the Decoder act provides for increased access to television programming for deaf people, the ADA established guidelines to end discrimination of disabled Americans and allow improved access to work and entertainment in the mainstream American society.

The ADA requires employers of 15 or more people to provide "reasonable accommodations" for disabled employees. This does not specifically require interpreters for deaf employees but can be understood to include interpreting services as well as TTY's, visual alarms and other devices or services. The ADA also established federal requirements for every state to provide telephone relay services available 24 hours a day and every day of the year without restrictions on the length or content of the calls. The ADA mandated that 911 emergency telephone services be accessible to TTY phone calls. Hotels had specific guidelines for providing TTYs and television caption decoding. One area with mixed results was that banks of pay phones with eight or more phones would be required to have one TTY-accessible pay phone for every eighth phone. The immediate result was that phone companies redesigned their public pay phone banks to contain no more than seven pay phones in a group.

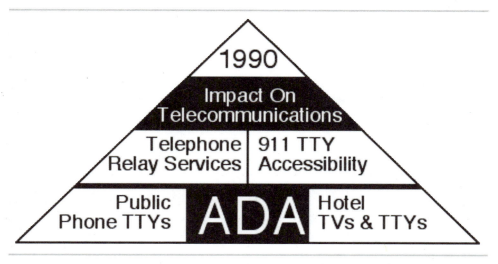

Figure 5.1 – Telecommunication Aspects of the ADA

Guidelines also require public business and services (including public performances) to be reasonably accessible. This does not require that every performance of a play have an interpreter nor that interpreters be available on call in every museum or courthouse. Instead the organizations and businesses offering public services must provide access *if requested in a timely manner*. Generally this has been understood as at least a two-week notice that interpreting services are preferred. Interpreting services are not necessarily required and so reasonable accommodations may come in the form of an audio loop system for enhanced sound or providing a copy of the script for a play. In doctors' offices and other businesses reasonable accommodation may mean writing information or providing a captioned training film.

The ADA requires the business or organization to be responsible for all related costs to providing accommodation. This is significant because it means that deaf patients cannot be billed for the costs of interpreting services during visits to the doctor or hospital. If the cost of providing reasonable accommodations is too expensive, the organization or business can avoid this responsibility by declaring them an "undue burden." The ADA legislation very carefully limits what constitutes an undue burden: the costs of the services are not to be compared to the money paid by the disabled consumers. Instead the overall budget of the business or organization must be used to determine undue burden. This means that even if the doctor charges $40.00 for an office visit and the interpreting services cost $50.00, it may not be an undue burden compared to the overall operating income and expenses of the doctor's office. The doctor is still required to pay for the accommodations and is not allowed to charge the deaf patient any more than other patients. Since the ADA does not specify that interpreters are the only reasonable accommodation for deaf consumers, it is still possible to avoid providing interpreting services so long as the alternatives are deemed "reasonable."

One concern that the Deaf community had about the ADA is that it provides for access based on them being considered disabled, rather than a linguistic and cultural minority. In other words, the law prohibits discrimination against Deaf people because they can't hear, not because they use signed language. While there is a certain stigma in accessing these rights by focusing on the disability of being unable to hear, the Deaf community has benefited greatly from the provisions of the ADA: most notably from the relay service which has empowered deaf people to conduct their own business rather than depending on relatives or neighbors to make phone calls for them.

While the ADA is important legislation to deaf Americans, it is important to remember that there are many provisions in the law for other disability groups. These include regulations regarding ramp access to stores and restaurants, parking spaces for handicapped drivers, and even the minimum width of doors and hand rails in public restrooms. The Deaf community acted together with veteran groups, organizations for blind people and people with cerebral palsy as well as other disability groups in order to ensure the passage of this landmark legislation for the Civil Rights of Disabled Americans.

The Television Decoder Circuitry Act

On October 16th, 1990, the federal government enacted the Television Decoder Circuitry Act, which mandated that all televisions (13" screens and larger) sold in the United States have built-in caption decoding capabilities as of July 1st, 1993. This act greatly increased the accessibility of captioning to people who might not be able to afford the additional expense of a separate caption decoder. This act also means that hotels and restaurants can easily provide caption access without purchasing additional equipment. As old televisions were replaced with new ones there was less and less need for separate caption decoding equipment and deaf people gained greater access through the same equipment as everyone else: no special assistive devices needed anymore in order to enjoy television. Within just a few years most televisions in public places (such as bars, restaurants, and hotels) were replaced with the newer televisions and this meant that Deaf people could request to have the captioning turned on (or often more effectively, just do it themselves). Some restaurants and bars became aware of the benefits of having captions on and the sound off.

With the increasing number of homes with caption capability there is now greater consumer pressure on broadcasters to caption their programming. In addition, the Federal Communications Commission (FCC) has been able to progressively increase the number of required weekly hours of captioned programming and by 2001 they had set forth a plan to require 100% of television broadcasts to be captioned by the year 2007.

Deaf Culture and Membership in the Deaf Community

Culture refers to the behavioral habits, communication, beliefs and artifacts of a community. Culture and language are tied together because for a language to exist, it must have a community of language users. For a community to exist, its members must communicate and language is one of the best transmitters of communication.

Deaf Culture includes the behavioral habits of using vision and touch extensively in human interaction and interaction with the environment; the use of Signed Languages for group face-to-face interaction and the use of written languages for distance communication through artifacts such as TTYs, caption decoders, fax machines, newspapers and magazines. The general similarities in belief center around perspectives of deaf people as capable people; and perspectives of American Sign Language as an efficient and effective language for members of the deaf community. This distinction between audiological deafness and cultural Deafness is marked by the use of a capitalized "D" to indicate the cultural meaning of Deaf. American Deaf culture thrives within the American deaf community.

The American Deaf Community consists of deaf people, hard of hearing people, and hearing people. Key factors that relate to membership include 1) fluency in American Sign Language, 2) political power in areas relevant to the deaf community, and 3) regular interaction within the community. "Core" membership is reserved for those who are deaf, fluent in ASL, have some political responsibilities within deaf-related organizations, and interact with the community at public and private events. Historically, deaf children of deaf parents who attended residential schools and were excellent story-tellers were the most likely to be considered within the "core."

Residential schools have historically played an essential role in the existence of deaf communities. With 90% of deaf children having hearing parents, most deaf children are not exposed to Deaf culture within their own homes. Residential schools have provided the means for deaf children and adults to congregate and transmit Deaf culture from one generation to the next. In this way residential schools have served as the cultural homes of deaf people. This is why the deaf community springs into action to prevent the efforts of school boards or state legislatures to close or reduce funding for a residential school.

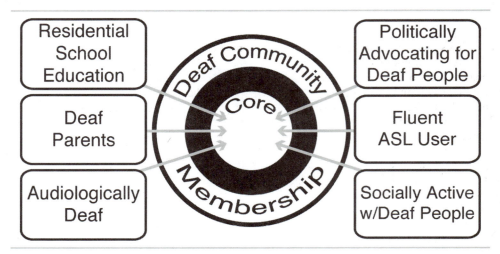

Figure 5.2 – Factors of Core Membership in the Deaf Community

It is certainly possible for hearing people to be members of the deaf community, become fluent in American Sign Language, and even to hold political office within deaf-related organizations. For this to be accomplished, a high level of interaction with the deaf community is required. It is essential that this interaction is motivated by the correct attitudes and expectations. The members of the deaf community are not seeking rescuers or people to save them from their situation. This attitude and its accompanying expectation of adoration and appreciation do not last long within the deaf community. Instead the deaf community seeks people who are connected by being deaf, being related to deaf people, or being friends to the deaf community.

Summary & Review Questions

Summary

This Unit presented the recent achievements of the Deaf community, from sports and theatre to the political arena, deaf people are doing for themselves what they want and need to do. While hearing people are certainly encouraged to work in partnership with the Deaf community, it is crucial to remember that the Deaf community serves its own needs best when it is in charge of providing the service. The Americans with Disabilities Act provides significant legal muscle to the deaf community, but unfortunately requires them to be labeled and perceived as disabled in order to access those rights.

Section 1 Review Questions

1)   What deaf sports organizations were formed in the 1900's?

2)   What notable sports achievements have been made by deaf people?

3)   What invention reduced the entertainment value of motion pictures for Deaf audiences?

4)   What kinds of controversy have been involved in portraying Deaf characters on television and in films?

5)   What kinds of films did Charles Kraul and Ernest Marshall each produce?

6)   What organization of Deaf Actors was formed in the 1960s?

7)   Why was the National Fraternal Society of the Deaf formed?

8)   What educational options for deaf students were created in the 1960s?

9)   What are some key differences between these schools?

Section 2 Review Questions

10)   What federal legislation has had an impact on the educational rights of Deaf students?

11)   What significance did the Deaf President Rally have on the outcome of the Deaf President Protests?

12)   How long did the DPN protests last?

13)   What were the four demands of the DPN protest?

14)   Who were the four student leaders of the DPN protest?

15)   What effect did the protests have upon campus life after they concluded?

16)   When and where were the Deaf Way conferences held?

17)   What kinds of events comprise Deaf Way conferences?

18)   What telecommunication advance was made for the Deaf community by a deaf person in 1964?

19)   When did closed captioning technology become available on national television broadcasts?

20)   What telecommunication rights are provided to Deaf people through the Americans with Disabilities Act?

21)   What did the Television Decoder Circuitry Act of 1990 require to take place by July of 1993?

22)   What qualities provide for greater acceptance (Core membership) in the Deaf community?

Bibliography & Suggested Readings

Deaf Community and Culture

Bragg, B. & E. Bergman. 1989. *Lessons in Laughter: The Autobiography of a Deaf Actor.* Washington, DC: Gallaudet University Press.

Bragg, B. & E. Bergman. 1981. *Tales From A Clubroom.* Washington, DC. Gallaudet College Press.

Crosby, O. 1995. *Silent Dancing: A Journey of Discovery.* Park City, UT: Osmond Crosby.

Eastman, G. 1997. *Sign Me Alice & Laurent Clerc: A Profile.* Dawn Sign Press.

Gannon, J. 1981. *Deaf Heritage: A Narrative History of Deaf America.* Silver Spring, MD: National Association of the Deaf.

Lane, H., R. Hoffmeister, & B. Bahan. 1996. *A Journey into the DEAF-WORLD.* San Diego, CA: Dawn Sign Press.

Neisser, A. 1983. *The Other Side of Silence: Sign Language and the Deaf Community in America.* Washington, DC: Gallaudet University Press.

Padden, C. and T. Humphries. 1988. *Deaf in America: Voices from a Culture.* Cambridge, MA: Harvard University Press.

Schuchman, J. S. 1989. *Hollywood Speaks: Deafness and the film Entertainment Industry.* Urbana, IL: University of Illinois Press.

Wilcox, S., Ed. 1992. *American Deaf Culture: An Anthology.* Burtonsville, MD: Linstok Press.

Deaf President Now

Christiansen, J. B. & S. N. Barnartt. 1995. *Deaf President Now! The 1988 Revolution at Gallaudet University.* Washington, DC: Gallaudet University Press.

Gannon, J. 1989. *The Week the World Heard Gallaudet.* Washington, DC: Gallaudet University Press.

Lane, H. 1992. *The Mask of Benevolence: Disabling the Deaf Community.* New York: Alfred A. Knopf.

Sacks, O. 1989. *Seeing Voices: A Journey into the World of the Deaf.* Berkeley, CA: University of California Press.

Interpreting in the Deaf Community

The weather was hot and muggy. I had been wearing the same clothes for two days, because the airline had sent my luggage to Chicago. People were beginning to keep a discreet distance from me. I would have avoided me too if I could have. That is my most vivid memory of the Workshop on Interpreting for the Deaf, held on the campus of Ball State Teachers College in Muncie, Indiana, June 14-17, 1964, during which the Registry of Interpreters for the Deaf (RID) was founded. ...

In my conversations and correspondence with some of the other participants, I am of the opinion that the occasion was not very dramatic nor exciting. It was not even a scheduled event on the agenda, and happened only because two participants, Edgar Lowell and Ralph Hoag, came up with the idea.

Lowell, then the Administrator of The John Tracy Clinic, knew no sign language and nothing about interpreting. He did, however, possess a keen mind and by questioning the participants, especially Hoag, the son of deaf parents and an accomplished interpreter, he acquired an understanding of the problems we were having in the field of interpretation. The major problem was the shortage of competent interpreters, so recruitment of interpreters and people to become interpreters were priority matters. (L. Fant, 1990: 1-2)

In 1964 the *profession* of sign language interpreting was born. Even in its origin, the RID included people on either side of the manualism-oralism debate; but as would happen decades later during the Deaf President Now protests, people on opposite sides of the issue joined forces for a common goal. The field has grown dramatically from its infancy – from zero interpreter training programs in 1964 to more than one hundred by 2000. Theoretical descriptive models of the work, ethical practices, certification standards, and continuing professional development have all developed in this time. This Unit reviews the history of the interpreting profession, its basic terminology and ethics, and its connections with the Deaf community.

Look for the answers to the following questions as you read:

1) What impact did the Nuremberg trials have upon future expectations of interpreting services?

2) How did electronics play a role in providing interpreting services at Nuremberg?

3) What is transcommunication and how do the following terms relate to each other?

    Translation

    Interpretation

    Transliteration

4) What is the difference between a source text and a target text?

5) How was the Registry of Interpreters for the Deaf established?

6) Why was the Registry of Interpreters for the Deaf established?

7) What role did the NAD play in the early years of the RID?

8) What are the eight tenets of the RID Code of Ethics?

9) How does an interpreter become certified?

10) What is the Triangle of Professionalism?

11) What are the educational requirements for maintaining RID Certification?

Section 1 – The Interpreting Process
The Nuremberg Trials

The history of interpreting will never be fully known. Ever since there have been people who wished to communicate, but did not share the same language, there has been a need for interpreters. Prior to the 1940's, most professional interpreting was done consecutively. This means that one person would produce a message (or part of a message) and then stop, momentarily, while the interpreter produced the same message (or part of the message) in another language. There was very little simultaneous interpreting happening at international business and political events because there was no easy access to private electronic sound systems. Without a private electronic sound system, a simultaneous interpretation would require that the speaker and the interpreter talk at the same time. This would be too distracting to the audience and the speaker. Widespread use of simultaneous interpreting would require a way of sending the interpretation to the listener without interrupting the main speaker.

It is often said that the mother of invention is necessity. When World War II ended and four major governments (the United States, England, France, and Russia) began investigating the activities of German leaders, it became necessary to interpret the proceedings in four languages: English, French, German, and Russian. Traditional (consecutive) approaches to interpreting between four languages would have extended the trial proceedings greatly. The need was for simultaneous interpreting; and the invention was a four-channel electronic sound system provided by IBM.[23]

When the Nuremberg Trials began, and judges from four different countries began to hear testimony regarding the war crimes of German leaders, a select group of people began providing simultaneous interpreting services. The procedures they developed would become the model for interpreting services at the United Nations and a wide variety of international events. Siegfried Ramler (1988) was one of the interpreters for the Nuremberg Trials, which began in 1946:

> We required teams of 12 interpreters for the trials, with three persons on each of four language microphones located in booths divided by glass panels. Thus the English channel would require one person to interpret from German into English, one from French in to English, and one from Russian into English. The same pattern continued for the other channels, so that, for example, the Russian booth would have three individuals translating from German into Russian, English into Russian and French into Russian. The eight members of the tribunal, the prosecution and defense staffs, the defendants and the audience in the courtroom wore earphones and were provided with a selector switch at each seat, allowing the listener to tune in to any of the four languages he wanted to hear. The original language spoken on the courtroom floor would, of course, come through "verbatim" on a given channel. This technology, with equipment which would be considered primitive by today's standards, was supplied by I.B.M. After the trial started, Hermann Goering was overheard to say: "This system is very efficient, but it will also shorten my life!" (Ramler, 1988: 437-438)

---

[23] This was actually an enhanced version of a six-channel device originally financed by Edward Filene and first used at the League of Nations in 1931.

In addition to providing simultaneous interpreting there were transcripts made of the proceedings in each language. Once interpreters had completed interpreting several hours of sometimes shocking testimony they had to verify the transcripts of their interpretations by comparing them with audio recordings of the trial. Even with all of this checking and double checking there were still disputes about the details of the interpretations, especially with terms which had rather neutral meanings in German but had taken on specific meanings under Nazi use: "A well-known example is the term 'Endlösung,' final solution, an innocuous term in ordinary use, but in the Nazi context indicating annihilation, as in 'the final solution of the Jewish problem.'" (Ramler, 1988: 439).

The importance of the interpreters' work was clearly appreciated by the people coordinating the trial. In post-World War II Germany there were great shortages of many things including motorized transportation, fuel, and food. Yet the interpreters were not only paid but were also provided with transportation, luxurious accommodations and good meals for the duration of the trial proceedings. The IBM technology would later be further enhanced and expanded to serve the needs of the United Nations where many of the practices established at the Nuremberg trials are still employed to this day.

The use of electronics to provide for efficient simultaneous interpretation in the Nuremberg trials has changed the face of interpreting. The interpreting process was previously (and accurately) perceived as a tedious and time-consuming process. It now is perceived to be a fairly effortless process, which is an unfortunate side-effect of the advances of technology. The process of interpreting remains just as tedious as it was before, but now the interpreter has even less time to do it because of technology. With the interpreter physically removed from their consumers, interpreters are now more likely to be forgotten and considered as part of that technology.

The use of microphones and headsets has provided the physical ability to generate an interpretation at the same time as the source text without interrupting it. The changes upon the resulting interpretation have been mostly negative because of the increased pressure on the interpreter, the reduction of the amount of time to process challenging portions of a source text, and the inability to interrupt the speaker. Interpreters used to work face to face with the members of their target language audience. Now the interpreters are placed in sound-proof booths, far from both the speaker and their audience. The advantages of saving time are counterbalanced by a reduction in the quality of the interpretation and the ability of the interpreter to convey the individual stylistics of the source speaker.

Removing the interpreters from the stage and hiding them behind the scenes in soundproof booths influenced how interpreters viewed their own work, much like the advent of oralism influenced the deaf community's view of themselves and their language. Paradigms of interpreting developed which reflected the notion that interpreters are to be invisible, unobtrusive, and make the communication exchange between two languages appear effortless. These expectations of interpreters influenced both spoken-language interpreters and signed-language interpreters. The rest of this unit will further explore the labels and technical terminology which defines the field of interpreting, then we will explore the Registry of Interpreters for the Deaf and its role in the profession of interpreting between English and ASL.

Transcommunication

Before we can move forward we need to define the word which captures all of the different kinds of work that can be done between languages and between Language Encoding Systems: Transcommunication.   **Transcommunication** is any kind of mediation where one person communicates another person's message to a third person. Transcommunication includes basic communication without using any language (such as waving to get someone's attention on behalf of another person), communication within a single language (such as reading a written message aloud to another person) and communication between two languages (such as translating information from one language to another).   We will begin with transcommunication without language, referred to here as *elucidation.*

There are many people who are faced with the need to communicate without sharing any common language between themselves and the people around them.   This can even be the case for locally available professional interpreters when a person's native language is not known to anyone locally or, in some cases, when a person is *not fluent in any language* at all.   In order to serve these people it is common practice to employ gestures and more dramatic enactment of the ideas that need to be conveyed.   Because the gesture does not constitute an actual language, none of the terms we will learn later in this chapter can be applied to this process of elucidation.   **Elucidation** is the transcommunication of a message between a language and something other than language.

Elucidation does not include communication between two people who use gestures to directly communicate with each other.   Such forms of communication may commonly take place in business exchanges where pointing gestures, written or signed numbers, and the exchange of money ensures sufficient communication to transact a sale between people who do not share any language.   Such direct exchanges of communication are not likely to be enhanced by a third person who also shares no language with either of the other two people.   Therefore we shall not further explore transcommunication that makes use of no languages whatsoever.

Elucidation as a process requires 1) a language user (or a linguistic text, such as a magazine article, an audio book, or a videotape), 2) a transcommunicator who knows the same language as the language user (or linguistic text), and 3) a non-language user, who must communicate without using a language.[24] A "linguistic text" is simply a document, which might be in a written language, such as a medical history form, or a signed language, such as a videotape.   An elucidator may read the medical history form, attempt to convey the items on the form gesturally (but not truly linguistically) to the non-language user.   Responses from the non-language user would then be written down by the elucidator.   This process is possible because communication *does not require* language; but the danger is that without language it is very difficult to be certain that the questions and answers are accurately understood.   Because languages are very refined forms of communication, transcommunication will always be more accurate when it makes use of language at both ends.

---

[24] People who know a language may need to communicate without language because they do not know any of the languages known by other people or because of an injury which prohibits natural language production or comprehension. It is also possible that the person is not fluent in any language at all.

Bilingual Transcommunication: Interpreting

One important thing to understand from the beginning is that there have been heated debates about just what professional interpreters are supposed to do in various situations and even about the basic definition of interpreting. Part of this argument has been the paradigm of "conduit" as a framework for understanding how an interpreter works. In the conduit framework, language is a package that contains ideas. On one end of communication people put their ideas "into" word packages. The words then travel somehow to other people who then "extract" meaning from the word packages and perhaps send a reply.

Within this framework, interpreters are one more handler of the package (the words). The notion is that the interpreter extracts the meaning from the words (the first container), finds equivalent words in the other language (a new container) and then sends the re-packaged message to the intended receiver. If everything goes smoothly, no one needs to know the interpreter was ever involved.

But this framework ignores the complexity of communication both through and beyond language. Eye contact, body posture, vocal intonation, and cultural expectations can all influence how we understand a message. Interpreters must include this kind of information in their interpretations. In other words, the interpreter not only replaces the container for the message (the words), but has to be concerned about how that container is wrapped (formal/informal; vocal inflection/facial expression), who is sending it, who is to receive it, how it is delivered, at what speed, and so forth. In addition to all of these factors, the very notion that a message can be "contained" or "packaged" into words is inaccurate since we know that communication requires background knowledge and a physical context. Every message is different and even multiple interpretations of the same message are possible, even necessary. Interpreting is a very interactive process that requires the interpreter to constantly make decisions.

So interpreters must understand information and do something with it. We will use the word "text" to refer to the information that a person produces. This includes the basic pieces of meaning as well as the cultural expectations surrounding the message and the manner in which it is delivered. Interpreters are working between two languages and cultures; therefore they work between two basic kinds of texts. **Source texts** are created by people other than the interpreter. **Target texts** are created by the interpreter. Figure 6.1 represents the sequence of a Source Text followed by a Target Text.

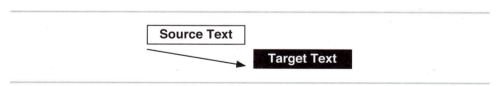

Figure 6.1 - Source and Target Texts

Another variable in describing texts is whether the texts are variable or fixed. **Variable texts** are spontaneously created and produced. **Fixed texts** are either prepared or recorded (by writing, audio recording, video recording or any other means of documentation).

It is possible to record a spontaneous, variable text. But the recording itself becomes a fixed text because it will be the same every time it is reviewed. One of the key factors to consider when determining whether a text is fixed or variable is the notion of being able to interrupt and redirect the message. It is not usually possible to interrupt a text written in a book or performed on videotape (other than to stop reading or to turn the VCR off). Modern innovations in interactive media, such as CD-ROMs and DVDs allow the viewer to interrupt and redirect the message so we need to introduce the other key factor: is the text the same each time it is presented? Each time a section of a CD-ROM or DVD is played it is the same as before (or one of a very few variations which will eventually repeat after several viewings). In other words, a person could memorize the patterns because they don't change. Books, CDs, DVDs, videotape, and any form of a recording are all examples of the ways that messages are fixed (made permanent).

Most of the time we would consider a live presentation to be spontaneous. Even if the person is performing in a play their performance is a spontaneous version of a fixed text because you could interrupt and ask a question. The performer may choose to ignore your interruption, but you might also get an answer (or a warning not to interrupt!) Live presentations are considered to be spontaneous texts.

With this understanding of what interpreters work with, we can now define the process of interpreting. **Interpreting is an interactive exchange of information between two languages in which the interpreter actively creates spontaneous target texts which maintain the information and intent of their respective variable source texts.** So if you thought interpreting was simple, now you know that it has a very complex definition. Let's examine the pieces one at a time.

1) *Interpreting is an interactive exchange of information.* This means that the interpreter is just as much involved in the exchange of information as every other person who is participating. In fact the interpreter usually participates exactly as much as every other person *combined*. Every message each person sends must be understood, analyzed, and regenerated by the interpreter.

2) *Interpreting exchanges information between two languages.* This may seem obvious now, but it is an essential part of the definition. Different labels apply to other kinds of work which exchange information within the same language.

3) *Interpreters actively create spontaneous target texts.* Our previous definitions indicated that interpreters are the people who create target texts but a key word related to *interpreting* is that the target text is spontaneously produced. If the target text is prepared or rehearsed and then recorded (written, typed, videotaped, etc), then we would probably call it a translation. In addition, the words "actively create" reveal that interpreters do not merely convey another person's thoughts. Interpreters must first bring their own knowledge and source language abilities to the understanding of the source texts. They then create their target texts based on that knowledge and their target language abilities.

4) *Interpreters maintain the information and intent of the source texts.* This means that the audience reaction to the interpretation should be the same as the reaction would be to the original message. This is tricky work because it requires the interpreter to make judgments about the meaning of the information and the speaker's intentions – often without being able to ask the speaker directly about what they thought the message meant and how they intended it.

To summarize, interpreting requires that two languages are involved. One language is related to the source text; the other language is related to the target text. The source text is variable and so is the target text. The process includes more than just repackaging words; it requires the interpreter to actively participate in the communication process. This means that no two interpreters will create identical target texts from the same source text.

Well, now that we know what interpreting is, and what it isn't, we can expand the definition even more. Within the realm of interpreting are two distinct forms. **Simultaneous Interpreting** occurs when the target text is created while the source text continues to be expressed. Simultaneous interpreting is common for monologic discourse, where one person will present a single source text (such as a lecture). Figure 6.2 indicates that the source text in one language begins before the target text in another language, which will be concluded just after the source text is complete.

Figure 6.2 - Simultaneous Interpretation of Monologic Discourse

Simultaneous Interpreting can also occur when two (or more) people interact with each other. Each target text is created while the source text continues to be expressed. Figure 6.3 indicates that the source text in one language begins before the target text in another language, which is then used to create another source text which is interpreted into the first language, and so on. Notice that there are time delays between the production of the source text and the production of the target text in both languages.

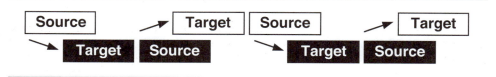

Figure 6.3 - Simultaneous Interpretation of Dialogic Discourse

The time delay between the source and target texts in each language can be problematic because the speaker who has just completed a source text may misunderstand the silence as an opportunity to take another turn. This means that the interpreter has to work to preserve the ability for the second language user to take a turn. This may mean that the interpreter explains the problem to the communicating parties. Other strategies exist for preserving the turn exchange, too. The main point here is that the interpreter must do more than merely "repackage" the message.

Consecutive Interpreting requires the production of the source text to be suspended while the target text is produced. Upon completion of the target text the next portion of the source text may be produced. Consecutive Interpreting is fairly common in settings where two or more people alternate in their creation of multiple source texts (such as a job interview). Figure 6.4 shows this typical patterns for consecutive interpreting of dialogic discourse.

Figure 6.4 - Consecutive Interpretation of Dialogic Discourse

Historically consecutive interpreting has also been done for monologic discourse but usually when the guest speaker (or business executive) is addressing a large audience which all share one language. This approach is only effective if the source text speakers agree to break-up their presentation into segments. Figure 6.5 shows this one-way use of consecutive interpreting for monologic discourse.

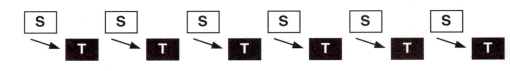

Figure 6.5 - Consecutive Interpretation of Monologic Discourse

Another word that has commonly been exchanged for "interpreting" is the word "translating"; but interpreting is not the same as translating. While interpreting depends on variable (non-fixed) source texts and the immediate creation of variable target texts, translation is a slower process which changes a fixed source text in one language into a fixed target text in another language. **Translation is the extensive review and evaluation of a fixed source text in one language and the creation of a fixed target text, in a different language, which maintains both the information and intent of the source text.** For example, a written English document may be reviewed and evaluated over the course of several days and an ASL version of the same information can be prepared and even recorded on videotape. It is possible to produce several drafts of the ASL version and choose one as the final translation of the original English text. The process may be similar or even identical to interpreting, but the key differences are 1) the source text is fixed, 2) the target text is fixed, and 3) there is sufficient time to review the source text and revise the target text.

Monolingual Transcommunication: Transliterating

Transliteration has traditionally meant the changing of letters in a word from one alphabet system to another. The point of transliteration is to allow a person who can read one alphabet access to a language that uses a different alphabet. Here is an example: If you went to Russia and encountered the words "POCTOb HA ΔONU" you would need to know the cyrillic alphabet in order to pronounce the words correctly. If I *transliterate* those words to "Rostov Na Donu" it still doesn't tell you what the words mean, but you now have access to the words through a *writing system* you know. Only when I tell you that this is the name of a town in South Western Russia and that it is generally written in English as "Rostov on Don" because it is on the Don River, do you understand its meaning because I have *translated* it into a *language* you know.

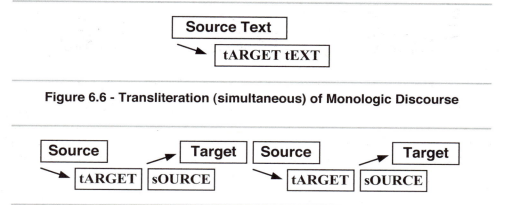

Figure 6.6 - Transliteration (simultaneous) of Monologic Discourse

Figure 6.7 - Transliteration (simultaneous) of Dialogic Discourse

The point to remember is that transliteration *does not cross the "language barrier."* That is, even though the form of the word, or words, have changed, the language remains the same. Unless you know that language, you will not be able to understand a text that has been transliterated from a form you do not have access to (such as cyrillic) to a form you do have access to.

The concept of transliteration has been expanded from its origins related to written languages to the presentation of spoken language in accessible forms for deaf people. Oral Transliteration is the presentation of spoken English into what has been called "Visible English" which is simply a controlled and clear presentation of lip movements, facial expression, and natural gesture which allows a deaf person with lip-reading skill to have access to the spoken language version. Both the source text and the target text are English.

Another version of transliteration is Cued Language Transliteration (generally known as Cued Speech). Cuing presents spoken language phonology through combinations of lip movement, eight handshapes, four locations, and six movement patterns, including epenthetic movement. Cued Language Transliteration makes use of the cuing system to present the phonology (speech sounds) of spoken languages to a consumer who also knows (or is learning) the cuing system. Once again, there is no change in language: both the source and target texts use the same language.

Transliteration also occurs with ASL. Deaf/blind people who attend conferences often receive either tactile or reduced-space transliteration when a source text is presented in ASL. Tactile transliteration/interpretation is used by deaf people who do not have usable vision. Reduced-space transliteration/interpretation is used by deaf people with limited usable vision such as tunnel vision. The interpreting versions of these will be presented when the source text is English. If the source text is ASL, then the task is transliteration, even though the end result looks the same. The key difference is whether the language barrier has been crossed. Many people who provide tactile or reduced-space transliteration for deaf/blind people are deaf themselves. They may use the services of an interpreter to take a spoken English text into ASL. This ASL text now becomes the source text for a tactile or reduced-space transliteration for deaf/blind consumers.

Notetaking is also a form of transliteration if it takes a spoken form of language and represents it in writing. Notes might be in shorthand, which is a phonetic representation of the source text, or in longhand (standard written English, for example). Notes could be typed or word-processed. The most technical of all transliterations is Computer Assisted Real-Time Transcription (CART), which starts with a phonetic encoding of a spoken language (much like the use of cues or shorthand) and then generates written English words and punctuation through computer software.

It is entirely possible for each of these forms of transliteration to be used as a part of interpreting. The determining factor is whether the language barrier is crossed. If so, then the act is one of interpreting. A German source text presented in lip-readable French would be an Oral Interpretation. A British Sign Language source text presented in cued English would be a Cued Language Interpretation. A Spanish source text presented in tactile ASL would be a Tactile Interpretation. An English source text presented in reduced-space ASL would be a Reduced-Space Interpretation. A Russian source text entered into a computer as encoding for spoken English and then processed by computer into written English would be a Computer Assisted Real-Time Transcription Interpretation. While all of these variations are possible, most of them do not occur very often. Tactile and Reduced-Space forms will be transliterations when the source and target languages are the same. They will be interpretations when the source and target languages are different.

Transcoding Natural and Artificial Pidgins

A Pidgin is a conglomerate of three or more languages used for interaction among people who otherwise do not share a common language. Pidgins do not meet the definition of language established in chapter one because they have yet to show historical change and be passed from one generation to another. Once the second generation has Creolized a Pidgin, the resulting Creole does indeed satisfy the definition of language. Therefore the following terminology correctly applies: Transcommunication between a language and a Creole is *Interpreting*. Transcommunication between a language and a Pidgin is not interpreting, but rather adopts the above-mentioned label of *Elucidation*.

In chapter four, we reviewed the reasons why manual English codes should be classified as Artificial Pidgins. Since Artificial Pidgins (ie. manual English codes) are not languages, neither the label *Interpreting* nor *Transliterating* can be correctly applied to any work that involves a manual English code. Therefore the label of *Elucidation* is all that can be correctly applied to any work involving a manual English code (such as SEE 2).

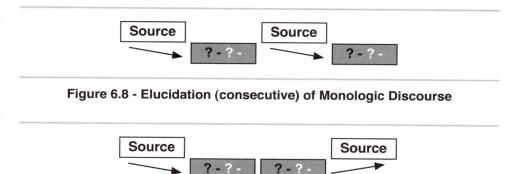

Figure 6.8 - Elucidation (consecutive) of Monologic Discourse

Figure 6.9 - Elucidation (consecutive) of Dialogic Discourse

Summary of Extralinguistic Transcommunication

Extralinguistic Transcommunication simply means that one side of the communication event did not use a language. In chapter one we introduced the concept of communication and the terms semiotics and pragmatics. Through semiotics it is possible to communicate without language. This may be accomplished through vocalizations, gestures, body postures and facial expression as well as graphic symbols. The key factor to consider is whether both kinds of communication are shared by members of a community in which the communication system is a) rule-governed, b) has infinite production possibilities, c) is intergenerational, and d) changes over time. If just one side of the communication event does not meet these requirements (such as the use of basic gestures, natural pidgins, or artificial pidgins) then any transcommunication between the two will be called Elucidation. If both sides of the communication even meet the definition of language then any transcommunication between the two will be described in the next sections of this chapter.

Section 2 – The Registry of Interpreters for the Deaf
The RID

There was a time, not long ago, when interpreters were not thought of as "professionals" – even by the people who were doing the interpreting. While foreign language conference interpreting had been widely regarded as professional work, community interpreting did not hold this status. Community interpreting with deaf people was seen as being charitable rather than anything professional.

Interpreting between a signed and spoken language as a profession has its origins in 1963 in Texas. The next year, a group of educators, interpreters, and rehabilitation counselors gathered at Ball State University in Muncie, Indiana between June 14 and June 17 in the summer of 1964. They had gathered for A Workshop on Interpreting but ended up establishing the roots for the Registry of Interpreters for the Deaf. A national organization of interpreters was proposed at the workshop and was established initially with the name "National Registry of Professional Interpreters and Translators for the Deaf."

The people providing interpreting services in 1964 were generally volunteers, providing services to friends and rarely reimbursed for their efforts at that time (Fant, 1990). This meeting was simply an attempt to solve the problem of identifying qualified interpreters nationwide but it ended up being the beginnings of the first national professional organization of Signed/Spoken Language Interpreters. It certainly was not regarded as historic by the people in attendance:

> In my conversations and correspondence with some of the other participants, I am of the opinion that the occasion was not very dramatic nor exciting. It was not even a scheduled event on the agenda, and happened only because two participants, Edgar Lowell and Ralph Hoag, came up with the idea.
> Lowell, then the Administrator of The John Tracy Clinic, knew no sign language and nothing about interpreting. He did, however, possess a keen mind and by questioning the participants, especially Hoag, the son of deaf parents and an accomplished interpreter, he acquired an understanding of the problems we were having in the field of interpretation. The major problem was the shortage of competent interpreters, so recruitment of interpreters and people to become interpreters were priority matters. Following hard on the heels of this would come the matter of training new recruits to become interpreters. Lowell and Hoag, then the administrator of the Grants-in-Aid Program for Training Teachers of the Deaf, U.S. Office of Education, agreed that some kind of organization seemed needed that could assess interpreter competency and maintain a registry of them so consumers could be assured of receiving quality service. (Fant, 1990: 1-2)

The meeting lasted two and a half hours and resulted in the election of an Executive Board which consisted of a President (Kenneth Huff, the superintendent of the Wisconsin School for the Deaf in Delevan, Wisconsin), a Vice President (Dr. Elizabeth Benson, the Dean of Women at Gallaudet College), a Secretary-Treasurer (Virginia Lewis of Youngstown, Ohio), and two members at large (Frank Sullivan of the National Fraternal Society of the Deaf, and Lillian Beard of Houston, Texas).

The five-member board took their positions as they were elected. Participants were asked to identify themselves as members of the new organization, if they desired, and if so to identify themselves as interpreters or as sustaining members. Forty-two of the participants identified themselves as interpreters and twenty-two others as sustaining members (although seven of these indicated that they could interpret). Thus began the National Registry of Professional Interpreters and Translators for the Deaf (NRPITD).

By the spring of 1965, the organization had changed its name to the Registry of Interpreters for the Deaf and was supported by a Rehabilitation Services Administration grant administered by the National Association of the Deaf (NAD). The NAD provided office space and support services through this time. This funding lasted until 1972 when the RID became an incorporated organization. The purpose of the organization had originally been to recruit, educate, and maintain an updated listing of signed language interpreters. The first national convention was held in Delevan, Wisconsin (where Wisconsin's residential school for deaf children is located) in 1970. Meetings were held every two years after that until 1982, then were shifted to odd-numbered years beginning in 1983. RID had grown in membership and also in scope: it is now concerned with certification standards and testing, certification maintenance through education, and the publication of research and theory related to the interpreting profession.

The RID is currently governed by a board of directors consisting of a president, vice-president, member-at-large, secretary/treasurer, and five regional representatives. The RID is managed on a daily basis by an executive administrator and the RID office staff. The National RID office is located in Silver Spring, Maryland which is also where the National Association of the Deaf has its national offices. The national office staff has specialized areas of responsibility for certification exams, certification maintenance, membership services, and publications.

The National Testing System (NTS) coordinator is responsible for ensuring the quality of the certification exams, the training of the raters, establishing testing sites, and scheduling and tracking candidates for certification. The Certification Maintenance Program (CMP) coordinator is responsible for coordinating the approval of educational offerings for Continuing Education Units (CEU's) in five categories of training, coordinating the sponsors of CMP educational offerings, and tracking the progress of all certified members toward maintaining their certification within the program. Membership Services maintains the list of RID members for publication in the annual RID membership directory, collects membership dues and issues membership cards. RID publications include the RID Views, which is the monthly newsletter containing reports from the board, regional representatives, and committees. It also lists upcoming certification exam testing dates, approved sponsors for the CMP, advertisements for interpreting products and employment, and articles of interest to the membership. The RID also publishes The Journal of Interpretation, which includes theory and research in the field of interpreting.

With approval of the national membership, the RID publishes various position papers, which reflect the official recommendations of the RID for various issues such as Team Interpreting, Mentoring, and Business Practices. There is also an Ethical Practices System (EPS) in place to review ethical practices of interpreters. This system allows consumers of interpreting services to file complaints about unethical interpreters. The review board has the authority to issue penalties to interpreters found to be in violation of the code of ethics, including the revocation of certification.

Within the membership of RID there are Special Interest Groups (SIGs) which can be formed either to address particular issues in the profession or to address specific groups of members. RID national conventions occur every odd-numbered year, while RID regional conventions occur every even-numbered year. Conventions provide the opportunity for the membership to propose and vote on motions during business meetings, attend educational workshops, and develop or strengthen professional contacts with other people in the field. The membership of RID consists of both certified and non-certified interpreters. Non-certified interpreters of RID are called Associate members and make up over half of the total membership in the RID.

RID's Code of Ethics

In order to practice a profession, some guidelines for proper professional behavior need to be established. The Registry of Interpreters for the Deaf has established such a code of ethics. The Canadian equivalent of the RID, AVLIC - the Association of Visual Language Interpreters of Canada, has a similar set of guidelines as well. The RID code of ethics has eight tenets, or points, which provide guidance and boundaries for the behavior of interpreters.

Tenet 1:	Interpreters / Transliterators shall keep all assignment-related information strictly confidential.
Tenet 2:	Interpreters / Transliterators shall render the message faithfully, always conveying the content and spirit of the speaker, using language most readily understood by the person(s) whom they serve.
Tenet 3:	Interpreters / Transliterators shall not counsel, advise, or interject personal opinions.
Tenet 4:	Interpreters / Transliterators shall accept assignments using discretion with regard to skill, setting, and the consumers involved.
Tenet 5:	Interpreters / Transliterators shall request compensation for services in a professional and judicious manner.
Tenet 6:	Interpreters / Transliterators shall function in a manner appropriate to the situation.
Tenet 7:	Interpreters / Transliterators shall strive to further knowledge and skills through participation in workshops, professional meetings, interaction with professional colleagues and reading of current literature in the field.
Tenet 8:	Interpreters / Transliterators, by the virtue of membership in or certification by the R.I.D., Inc., shall strive to maintain high professional standards in compliance with the code of ethics.

RID Code of Ethics 1979-2004

> **Interpreters have a professional responsibility to:**
>
> **Tenet 1:** Adhere to standards of confidential communication.
>
> **Tenet 2:** Possess interpreting competence commensurate with the communication event.
>
> **Tenet 3:** Actively engage in ongoing professional development.
>
> **Tenet 4:** Demonstrate respect for all consumers and their diversity.
>
> **Tenet 5:** Demonstrate respect for the profession, other colleagues, and students of the profession.
>
> **Tenet 6:** Render services linguistically accessible and appropriate for the situation.
>
> **Tenet 7:** Conduct themselves in a manner befitting the assigned setting.
>
> **Tenet 8:** Ensure that working conditions are conducive to excellence in service delivery.
>
> **Tenet 9:** Serve as a resource on interpreting and relevant services, as needed.
>
> **Tenet 10:** Maintain ethical business practices.

RID Code of Ethics (adopted 2004)

These tenets of the code of ethics define what behavior is appropriate and expected for interpreters. They allow consumers of interpreting services know what an interpreter should be expected to do and what should not be expected. More than anything else, they protect the interpreter from getting into responsibilities they are not prepared for. If an interpreter provides advice, but is not qualified to give the advice, then the interpreter may be liable for misleading, misinforming, or manipulating the deaf or hearing consumers. Keeping information confidential protects the consumers as well as the interpreter. If private information, learned during an interpreting assignment, is released to the community by the interpreter, other consumers may learn not to trust that interpreter and may refuse to use that interpreter's services again. If the interpreter accepts work that is clearly beyond the interpreter's ability then the potential misinformation that ensues may lead to legal problems for both the consumer and the interpreter. While there will be occasions when we break the code of ethics, they are there to remind us of the goals for ethical behavior and allow us to understand potential problems and work to reduce the number of ethical errors we make as we continue to work in our profession.

RID Certification

In order to establish standards of interpreting performance, the Registry of Interpreters for the Deaf (RID) has established evaluation and certification procedures. Certification indicates a minimal level of acceptable skill - it is not an indication of perfection. Once members of RID have achieved certification, they must continue to educate themselves through the Certification Maintenance Program (CMP) which requires an average of 20 contact hours of continuing education every year.

The original certification procedures were implemented in 1972 and involved a live panel of judges who would ask questions regarding ethics and interpreting practices and also observe various interpreting performances. Candidates would receive scores from each judge and also receive various kinds of certification, depending upon the score averages. The top certificate was the Comprehensive Skills Certificate (CSC) which indicated that the candidate could adequately interpret English messages to ASL, ASL messages to English, contact ASL to English, and English to contact ASL.

If the candidate could do all of the above but to a lesser level of quality or skill, then the candidate could receive a partial certification of IC/TC (IC = Interpreter Certification, TC = Transliterator Certification). If the candidate did only one of these areas well, then the candidate would receive either the IC or the TC. Any lesser skill levels received no certification.

In addition to these certifications, deaf people could also receive certification. By successfully taking ASL or contact ASL into English (which required the deaf person to have intelligible speech) the deaf candidate could receive an RSC, or Reverse Skills Certificate. There were certification procedures for Oral Transliteration (at that time called Oral Interpreting) which yielded either an OIC:C (Oral Interpreter Certificate: Comprehensive), an OIC:S/V (Oral Interpreter Certificate: Spoken to Visible), or an OIC:V/S (Oral Interpreter Certificate: Visible to Spoken).

There was a Specialist Certificate in Performing Arts (SC:PA), a Specialist Certificate in Legal interpreting (SC:L) and for a few people, a Masters Comprehensive Skills Certificate (MCSC) which indicated that the person's skills were at a higher, more experienced level than required for the CSC.

These procedures of certification had lead to a perception that some panels were harsher than others in judging candidates. Some people who had received CSC's in rural areas had skills that (some people believed) wouldn't have been awarded any certification at all in the more metropolitan areas of California or New York. There was a general need to standardize the test nationwide and provide consistency. There was also the reality that issuing "partial" certification was not truly professional (how many *partially* certified teachers or *partially* certified physicians do you know?)

In 1989 the new RID evaluation and certification system was put into place. The new system involves completing a written exam on ethics and interpreting history and practices. Upon successful completion of this step, the candidate has five years before they must complete one (or both) of two certification performance examinations: the CI exam for the Certificate of Interpretation, and the CT exam for the Certificate of Transliteration. This five-year period will eventually need to shrink to a one-year period in order to conform with the certification procedures of other professionals. This five-year period has been misunderstood as being a time to further develop skills prior to taking the performance exam. In truth, the candidate should be ready to take and pass all portions of the certification exam before taking the written exam.

For either performance exam the candidate receives one hour and fifteen minutes of warm-up time. During this time a Local Test Administrator (LTA) reviews the testing procedures and then allows the candidate time to review videotapes relevant to the testing material. The test consists of three segments, each lasting about twenty minutes. Two segments are lectures: one in ASL (or linear ASL) which the candidate must interpret to English, known as Sign to Voice (or S-V), the other in spoken English with the candidate interpreting into ASL (or linear ASL), known as Voice to Sign (or V-S). The remaining segment is a one-to-one interview (1-1) in which a deaf and hearing person have a conversation regarding professional services (ie. the hearing person is the professional and the deaf person is getting advice or other services from the hearing person). The candidate must render the deaf person's utterances into spoken English, and the hearing person's spoken utterances into signed ASL (or contact ASL).

In the warm-up room the candidate views tapes of the same people on the test talking about related topics (well, almost always related topics). The candidate has two choices of people for each segment (A or B) and can choose any configuration of the test in any order that they want. Their final configuration for the test may be 1-1:A, V-S:B, and S-V:B, for example. Once the warm up is complete and the candidate has chosen which options will make up the test then each segment is videotaped with a five-minute break between each part. The resulting tape is then sent to three groups of raters (deaf, hearing (who know no sign), and interpreters). Each group must pass the tape in order for the candidate to receive either the CI or the CT.

The Triangle of Professionalism

Certification is one significant part of a profession. The other two parts are an Ethical Practices Review system, whereby the behaviors of professionals can be challenged to ensure that they are behaving ethically in their provision of services, and Certification Maintenance, whereby members of the profession demonstrate that they are continuing their education regarding current practices in the field. In 1972 RID began to venture toward true professionalism with its Certification System. In the 1980's an Ethics Grievance system was in place for a while but was not re-established until the mid 1990's. In 1994, the Certification Maintenance System was finally put into action, thereby completing the three corners of the Triangle of Professionalism. These elements are represented in the graphic below:

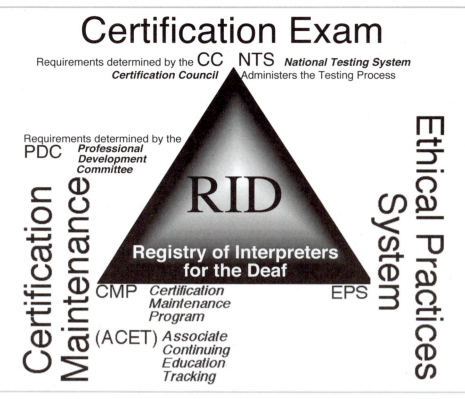

Figure 6.10 – The Triangle of Professionalism

RID's Certification Maintenance Program

Once an interpreter receives national certification from the RID, they must earn Continuing Education Units (CEUs) to maintain their certification. These CEUs are arranged through RID's Certification Maintenance Program (CMP) which was established in 1994. If interpreters do not earn the required number of RID CEUs then they will lose their certification. Interpreters who lose their certification in this manner can only become certified again by taking the certification exam for each certificate desired.

Originally the CMP required 90 hours of training in every three-year cycle. These requirements were reduced in 1999 when it was discovered that the average level of certified interpreters had increased since 1994 when the initial requirements were established. The current requirement is an average of twenty contact hours of continuing education per year. Every ten hours of training is considered as 1.0 CEUs. Under current requirements a certified interpreter is required to have 8.0 CEUs every four years.

There are two categories for the CEUs: Professional Studies (PS) and General Studies (GS). Professional Studies relates to any work that directly relates to interpreting. General Studies relates to all other learning. RID Certified members are required to attain a minimum of 6.0 CEUs in the Professional Studies category within each four-year cycle. The remaining required CEUs may also be Professional Studies, General Studies, or any combination of the two.

CEUs can only be awarded through RID-approved Continuing Education Sponsors. All activities for CEUs must be approved by sponsors prior to the activity. It is not possible to request CEUs for a learning activity after the learning has already taken place. Some sponsors offer independent study options that allow up to 2.0 CEUs for each project. Independent studies typically involve reading some material related to interpreting and then writing a summary report or participating in an interview with the sponsor to determine that the information was learned and applied to professional growth.

College courses also count for CEUs. College courses earn CEUs based on the number of contact hours and are not considered independent studies (therefore they are not limited to 2.0 CEUs). Interpreter trainers may also earn CEUs for their efforts in preparing a course or workshop the first time it is offered. It has become a standard practice that workshops and conferences offered specifically for interpreters will have all of their training sessions approved for CEUs. Business meetings do not count as professional training. There is no requirement that all training be approved for CEUs so contact the coordinators of the event to be certain that CEUs are offered.

As an example lets consider two interpreter. Pat is certified for Oral Transliteration (OTC), Interpreting (CI), "Transliterating" (CT), and Legal interpreting (SC:L). Chris is certified only for Oral Transliteration. Pat holds four certifications with RID while Chris holds only one certification. They both must earn the same number of CEUs within each four-year cycle. Chris lives near an interpreting program and takes two advanced three-credit, semester-based courses. These courses provide 45 contact hours each and therefore each course is worth 4.5 CEUs in the Professional Studies area. At the end of just one semester Chris has 9.0 CEUs and has already exceeded[25] the required number of CEUs for the current four-year cycle.

Pat lives in a rural area and can rarely go to workshops and conferences. Pat knows that if the required number of CEUs is not earned then all four certifications are at risk. Pat opts to use the independent study option to earn CEUs. Pat reads books and writes essays, through the approval of a sponsor for independent studies. Pat earns the required number of CEUs within two and a half years and keeps all four certifications current into the next cycle. If Pat did not met the requirements then all four certifications would be lost and could only be regained by taking the test for each of the four certifications.

The purpose of the Certification Maintenance Program is to provide an assurance that interpreters do not stop their education upon certification. Since requiring recertification every four years would be expensive and burdensome to the certification system, *maintenance* was chosen instead. Other professions require continuing education to maintain certification including physicians, nurses, financial planners and many other kinds of professional service providers.

Because the profession of interpreting is still relatively new, there are few states that have any educational requirements to become an interpreter. This means that it is possible for some interpreters to have Ph.D.s while others have not even graduated from

---

[25] NOTE – It is not possible to "roll over" extra CEUs from one four-year cycle to the next.

high school. The current educational requirements in the CMP are fairly high compared to professions that require a Masters degree or a Doctorate but are comparable to other professions that do not have high degree requirements to enter the profession. As entrance requirements to the interpreting profession rise, the number of CEUs required to maintain RID certification will be reduced.

Sampling of College Courses
Which Should Satisfy Requirements as RID PROFESSIONAL STUDIES

ANT	Anthropology	ITP	Interpreter Training Program
ASL	American Sign Language	JRN	Journalism
BUS	Business	LAT	Latin Language & Culture
CRT	Court Reporting	MMC	Multimedia Communications
ENG	English Writing & Literature	PSY	Psychology
FCL	Foreign Culture & Language	RUS	Russian Language & Culture
FRE	French Language & Culture	SOC	Sociology
GER	German Language & Culture	SPA	Spanish Language & Culture
ITA	Italian Language & Culture	SPH	Speech

Summary & Review Questions

Summary

This Unit presented the beginning of spoken-language interpreting as a profession (the 1946 Nuremberg trials) and of signed-language interpreting (the 1964 meeting at Ball State in Muncie Indiana). The rest of the chapter explored the definitions of terminology in the field of interpreting, and the specific requirements of the RID to maintain professional status in the field of interpreting (the Triangle of Professionalism, Certification, Ethics Review, and Certification Maintenance).

Section 1 Review Questions

1) What languages were interpreted at the Nuremberg trials?

2) What kind of interpreting did the Nuremberg trials require in order to be accomplished as quickly as they were?

3) What kind of electronic device was used in conjunction with the interpreting at Nuremberg?

4) Define the following terms:

Source Text	Target Text
Translation	Transliteration
Interpreting	Transcommunication

Section 2 Review Questions

5) What year was the RID founded?

6) What year did the RID begin certifying interpreters?

7) What are the full names of the following RID certifications (which are old, which are current)?

CI	CT	IC	TC	CSC
OIC	SC:L	SC:PA	RSC	OTC

8) How many tenets are in each of the old and new RID Code of Ethics?

9) Identify at least four tenets of the current RID Code of Ethics.

10) How many contact hours equal one CEU in the RID Certification Maintenance Program?

11) How many CEUs are required in every RID CMP cycle?

12) Name four different kinds of college courses that would be considered Professional Studies under the RID CMP requirements.

Interpreting

Baker, Mona. 1993. *In Other Words*. New York, NY: Routledge.

Bonvilliam, N. 1993. *Language, Culture, and Communication: The Meaning of Messages (Second Edition)*. Upper Saddle River, NJ: Prentice Hall.

Cerney, B. 1996. "Language Acquisition, Language Teaching, and the Interpreter as a Model for Language Input" *RID 1995 National Convention Proceedings*. Silver Spring, MD: RID Publications.

Cokely D. 1992. *Interpretation: A Sociolinguistic Model*. Burtonsville, MD: Linstok Press.

Cokely D. (Ed.) 1992. *Sign Language Interpreters and Interpreting*. Burtonsville, MD: Linstok Press.

Crabtree, M. & J. Powers, Eds. *Language Files: Materials for an Introduction to Language*. Columbus Ohio: Ohio State University Press.

Fant, L. 1990. *Silver Threads: A Personal Look at the First Twenty-five Years of the Registry of Interpreters for the Deaf*. Silver Spring, MD: RID Press.

Fant, L. 1983. *The American Sign Language Phrase Book*. Chicago, IL: Contemporary Books, Inc.

Fleetwood, E., & M. Metzger. 1990. *Cued Speech Transliteration: Theory and Application*. Silver Spring, MD: Calliope Press.

Frishberg, N. 1990. *Interpreting: An Introduction*. Silver Spring, MD: RID Press.

Gebron J. 1996. *Sign the Speech: An Introduction to Theatrical Interpreting*. Hillsboro, OR: Butte Publications, Inc.

Humphrey J. & B. Alcorn. 1994. *So You Want to Be an Interpreter: An Introduction to Sign Language Interpreting*. Salem, OR: Sign Enhancers, Inc.

Kaplan, H, S. Bally, & C. Garretson. 1985. *Speechreading: A Way to Improve Understanding*. Washington, DC: Gallaudet University Press.

McIntire, M. 1986. *Interpreting: The Art of Cross Cultural Mediation - Proceedings of the Ninth National Convention of the Registry of Interpreters for the Deaf July 4-8, 1985*. Silver Spring, MD: RID Publications.

RID. 1996. *RID 1995 National Convention Proceedings*. Silver Spring, MD: RID Publications.

RID. 1995. *A Confluence of Diverse Relationships: Proceedings of the Thirteenth National Convention of the Registry of Interpreters for the Deaf August 10-14, 1993*. Silver Spring, MD: RID Publications.

Seal, B. C. 1998. *Best Practices in Educational Interpreting*. Needham Heights, MA: Allyn & Bacon.

Seleskovitch D & M. Lederer. 1978. *A Systematic Approach to Teaching Interpretation*. Washington, DC: Pen and Booth.

Seleskovitch D. 1989. *Interpreting for International Conferences: Problems of Language and Communication*. Silver Spring, MD: RID Publications.

Solow S.N. 1981. *Sign Language Interpreting: A Basic Resource Book*. Silver Spring, MD: National Association of the Deaf.

Deaf Organizations in the United States

National Deaf Community Organizations

AADB	American Association of the DeafBlind
AAAD	American Athletic Association of the Deaf
AGBAD	Alexander Graham Bell Association for the Deaf
ALDA	Association of Late Deafened Adults
ASDC	American Society for Deaf Children
ASLTA	American Sign Language Teachers Association
BDA	Black Deaf Advocates
CAID	Convention of American Instructors of the Deaf
CAN	Consumer Action Network
CIT	Conference of Interpreter Trainers
CSUN	California State University at Northridge
GUAA	Gallaudet University Alumni Association
NAD	National Association of the Deaf
NCOD	National Center on Deafness (Northridge, CA)
NCSA	National Cued Speech Association
NFSD	National Fraternal Society of the Deaf
NTD	National Theatre for the Deaf
NTID	National Technical Institute for the Deaf
RID	Registry of Interpreters for the Deaf
SHHH	Self Help for the Hard of Hearing
TDI	Telecommunications for the Deaf, Inc.
WFD	World Federation of the Deaf

Course ID:	**ASL 110 - «SectionNumber»**	
Course Title:	**History of the Deaf Community**	
Room Location:	**«Location»**	
Meeting Times:	**«MeetingTimes»**	
Cancellation Info:	**«Info»**	
Instructor:	**«TeacherID»**	
Office Hours	**By appointment**	**«EMail»**

Required Course Materials:

- Cerney, Brian. 2005. Deaf History Notes. Colorado Springs, CO: Hand & Mind Publishing. ISBN: NONE
- Crosby, Osmond. 1995. Silent Dancing: A Journey of Discovery. Park City, Utah: Osmond Crosby. ISBN: NONE (Available through Cued Speech Discovery Bookstore, Cuedspdisc@aol.com
- Padden, C., & T. Humphries. 1988. Deaf in America: Voices from a Culture. Cambridge, MA: Harvard University Press. ISBN: 0-674-19423-3
- Van Cleve, John & Barry Crouch. 1989. A Place of Their Own: Creating the Deaf Community in America. Washington, DC: Gallaudet University Press. ISBN: 0-930323-49-1

Evaluations:

Attendance and Participation	100 points
Six Unit Exams [based on lectures] (15 points each)	90 points
Five Reading Quizzes [based on book readings] (20 points each)	100 points
One Comprehensive Final Exam [based on readings & lectures]	100 points
Six reaction papers [to Deaf Life articles] (10 points each)	60 points
Five film reviews (10 points each)	50 points
One Article Summary Outline (5 pts) & Presentation (5 pts)	10 points
Total Point Value	**510 points**

91 - 100%	451 - 510 = A Excellent
81 - 90%	401 - 450 = B Above Average
71 - 80%	351 - 400 = C Average
60 - 70%	300 - 350 = D Below Average

Course Goals:

The deaf experience is similar in many ways to the experience of many oppressed populations. Unique to the deaf experience is the mode of communication and the desire of hearing people to "fix problems" associated with deafness. This course will provide an in-depth investigation into the deaf experience. Specifically this course will focus on historical aspects of Deaf people and apply that knowledge to understand the attitudes and expectations of Deaf people today.

Sample Course Outline for "History of the Deaf Community"

Course Requirements
Attendance and Participation (100 Points):
The Attendance and Participation Form reviews student behavior and generates a score between 0 and 100 points. Indicators of Exemplary Performance include the following:
• attended every class on time, did not linger after breaks or leave early
• highly motivated to learn, actively engaged in course activities, did not participate in side conversations
• always prepared, motivated to begin and complete independent tasks, completed all assignments on time
• communicated appropriately / visually at all times, cooperated with both teacher and peers
• motivated to participate in or volunteer for activities, clearly enjoyed being in class

Unit Exams (90 Points):
Six organized lectures are presented, beginning with the first day of class. Lectures review material presented in the "Deaf History Notes" handout supplied by the instructor. Students are encouraged to read this material before class, highlight areas of significance reviewed in the lectures, and take additional notes. Unit exams must be completed from memory (no notes allowed during the test). Each exam is short-answer, requiring the student to provide a brief explanation in response to each question. Students who miss a Unit Exam on its assigned date may take a make-up exam on the next scheduled day of class. After that time, it is not possible to make-up the points lost on a Unit Exam. If you know that you will miss a testing date, please make arrangements before the absence to take the make-up exam, either before your anticipated absence or on the class session immediately after the assigned testing date.

Reading Quizzes (100 Points):
Quizzes on Reading Assignments. Three books are required reading for this course. Each quiz is short-answer, requiring the student to provide a brief explanation in response to each question. Students are permitted to use their notes while taking the quizzes; therefore students are encouraged to take detailed notes on each text. The Van Cleve & Crouch text has three quizzes. The Padden & Humphries text has one quiz. The Oz Crosby text also has only one quiz. In order to allow students to prepare, Quizzes on Reading Assignments are generally on different dates than the Unit Exams. Students who miss a Reading Quiz on its assigned date may take a make-up quiz on the next scheduled day of class. After that time, it is not possible to make-up the points lost on a Reading Quiz. If you know that you will miss a testing date, please make arrangements to take the reading quiz, before your anticipated absence.

Comprehensive Final Exam (100 Points):

The Final Exam covers all the material from the Deaf History Notes document (whether it was previously tested or not) and material previously covered in reading quizzes. Students are encouraged to take notes during the review session, but the Final Exam must be completed from memory (no notes allowed). Each question is short-answer, requiring the student to provide a brief explanation in response to each question. IT IS NOT POSSIBLE TO TAKE THE FINAL EXAM AFTER ITS SCHEDULED DATE. If you know that you will miss the testing date, please make arrangements to take the Final Exam PRIOR to your anticipated absence.

Reaction Papers (60 Points):

Articles for reaction papers will be distributed the first day of class. Reaction papers are not research papers nor are they summaries. They are one or two pages which document your feelings, your thoughts, and your insight about a magazine article. Each article presents issues specific to the deaf community but you should look into your own past or present to find experiences of your own or of people you know which in some way parallel those experiences of the people or topics discussed in each article. Reaction papers should 1) analyze the issue as the author presents it, 2) reveal whether the information was new or old to you, 3) indicate how it might have changed your thinking about an issue, 4) identify where you agree with the author and where you disagree, and 5) consider how the issue may relate to other minority groups. [2 points are awarded for each of these five areas... please label them clearly] Reaction papers may be submitted early, and students are encouraged to complete them ahead of their scheduled times. Papers submitted after the identified due date will have an automatic 5-point deduction. Papers will not be accepted after the class session before the Final Exam.

Film Reviews (50 Points):

Five films on videotape are ON RESERVE and available for viewing within the Allegheny, North and Boyce campus libraries. The first Film Review is "My Third Eye" (MTE) which will be treated differently from the other three films. Film Reviews may be submitted early, and students are encouraged to complete them ahead of their scheduled times. Film Reviews submitted after the identified due date will have an automatic 5-point deduction. Film Reviews will not be accepted after the class session before the Final Exam.

• For My Third Eye, describe each scene, what the actors do, and what each scene reveals about the deaf community and/or sign language.

• For the remaining four films, write a two page review of each film. Describe 1) the plot or story of the film, 2) the perspectives of deafness presented by the hearing people in the film, 3) the perspectives of deafness held by the deaf people in the film, 4) how those perspectives provide conflict, and 5) in what ways that conflict is resolved in the film. [2 points are awarded for each of these five areas... please label them clearly]

Article Summary Reports (10 Points):
Articles for Summary Reports are provided by the instructor. Presentations are biographical and report on a person of some significance to the American Deaf community. Only one student may report on any single cover story. Presentations require a two-to-five minute presentation to the class [scored as part of Attendance and Participation] (either from memory or from notes) and a one-page outline to be submitted to the instructor immediately prior to the beginning of your presentation. Students must not read a prepared presentation, however they may use notecards to remind them of their main points. Student presentations will occur from time to time as determined by the instructor. Students who are prepared early may positively influence their Attendance and Participation scores. If extra articles are available, students may present an additional presentation (with outline) worth ten bonus points.

In-class Videos: A significant portion of this class is dedicated to viewing short videos (usually a half-hour or less each). These videotapes have been selected to provide an enhanced understanding of topics covered in the course. Students are encouraged to take notes, but the only elements of videotapes that will appear on exams or quizzes are those which also appear in the written materials and/or lectures.

Student Preparation: In order to accomplish these goals and maximize the learning potential of classroom activities, the student is expected to read the material provided in their textbooks and supplemental handouts BEFORE those topics are covered in class. Students must find time to view the four films for the Film Reviews. Two copies of each film is on reserve in both the North Campus Library and the Boyce Campus Library. Only one of the videos, "Children of a Lesser God", is otherwise widely available for rental or purchase.

Session # & Dates:	Activities For All Sections	
Session #1 «DayandDate1»	Distribution of all readings / Course Overview Video - Spin City episode with Marlee Matlin Video - Sicard & Massieu	Unit 1 Lectures
Session #2 «DayandDate2»	Reaction Paper #1 due: "What do We Call Ourselves?" Video - In the Land of the Deaf Discussion of Reaction Paper #1	Unit 1 Exam
Session #3 «DayandDate3»	• Reading Quiz #1 from notes on Van Cleve & Crouch pp 1 - 46 • Video - The Milan Conference Video - Preservation of the Sign Language	Unit 2 Lectures
Session #4 «DayandDate4»	Reaction Paper #2 due: "Junius Wilson" Video - The Ear Video - Deaf Mosaic: Cochlear Implants Discussion of Reaction Paper #2	Unit 2 Exam Unit 3 Lectures

Session #5
«DayandDate5»

• Reading Quiz #2 from notes on Van Cleve & Crouch pp 47 - 105 •
Reaction Paper #3 due: "Cochlear Implants"   More Unit 3 Lectures
Video - Koko / 48 Hours
Video - Lynn Baker Interview Highlights
Discussion of Reaction Paper #3

Session #6
«DayandDate6»

Reaction Paper #4 due: "Deafness as Culture"   Unit 3 Exam
Video - Charles Kraul   Unit 4 Lectures
Video - Ernest Marshall
Video - Bonnie Kraft Segments
Discussion of Reaction Paper #4

Session #7
«DayandDate7»

• Reading Quiz #3 from notes on Van Cleve & Crouch pp 106 - 174 •
Reaction Paper #5 due: "Faking It"   More Unit 4 Lectures
Video - Adventures in Cued Speech
Video - DPN Rally (March 1st, 1988)
Discussion of Reaction Paper #5

Session #8
«DayandDate8»

Film Review #1 due: "My Third Eye"   Unit 4 Exam
Video - Rainbow's End - Dr. Plural   Unit 5 Lectures
Video - Marlee Matlin Oscar Award
Video - DPN Protests (March 6-13, 1988)

Session #9
«DayandDate9»

Reaction Paper #6 due: "Deaf President Now"   More Unit 5 Lectures
Video - Deaf Mosaic "Deaf President Now"   Student Presentations
Discussion of Reaction Paper #6

Session #10
«DayandDate10»

Film Review #2 due: "Love is Never Silent"   More Unit 5 Lectures
Video - Deaf Mosaic "The Deaf Way"   Student Presentations
Video - Deaf Mosaic "DPN - Five Years After"

Session #11
«DayandDate11»

Film Review #3 due: "Children of a Lesser God"   Unit 5 Exam
Video - Star Trek "Loud As a Whisper"   Unit 6 Lectures

Session #12
«DayandDate12»

Film Review #4 due: "Bridge to Silence"   More Unit 6 Lectures
• Reading Quiz #4 from notes on Padden & Humphries Book (pp 12 - 121)

Session #13
«DayandDate13»

Film Review #5 due: "Sound And Fury"   Unit 6 Exam

Session #14
«DayandDate14»

• Reading Quiz #5 from notes on Oz Crosby book pp 1 – 142 •
Deaf Trivia Game
Review for Final

Session #15
«DayandDate15»

COMPREHENSIVE FINAL EXAM

Student Attendance & Participation Form

Student Name: _____ **Date:** ___/___/___ **Score:**_____
Instructor(s): _____ **Course:** _____
This form is completed by instructor during the last week of the course.

__ **100) Exemplary Student**
- attended every class on time, did not linger after breaks or leave early
- highly motivated to learn, actively engaged in course activities, did not participate in side conversations
- always prepared, motivated to begin and complete independent tasks, completed all assignments on time
- communicated appropriately / visually at all times, cooperated with both teacher and peers
- motivated to participate in or volunteer for activities, clearly enjoyed being in class

__ **90) Excellent Student**
- occasionally late to class, late from breaks, left early OR missed one class
- motivated to learn material, actively engaged in course activities
- always prepared, motivated to begin and complete independent tasks, completed all assignments on time
- inappropriately spoke with peers during class time, but otherwise cooperated with both teacher and peers
- generally motivated to participate in or volunteer for activities, clearly enjoyed being in class

__ **80) Above Average Student**
- occasionally late to class, late from breaks, left early OR missed one class
- motivated to learn course material, actively engaged in course activities
- usually prepared, motivated to begin and complete independent tasks, completed all assignments on time
- inappropriately spoke with peers during class time, but otherwise cooperated with both teacher and peers
- willing to participate in discussions or activities when selected by teacher

__ **70) Average Student**
- often late to class / late from breaks / left early OR missed two classes
- usually motivated to learn course material, but occasionally disengaged from course activities
- usually motivated to begin and complete independent tasks, completed almost all assignments on time
- often forgot to communicate appropriately / visually with teacher, often participated in side conversations
- willing to participate in discussions or activities when selected by teacher

__ **60) Below Average Student**
- repeatedly late to class / late from breaks / left early OR missed three classes
- not motivated to learn course material and often disengaged from course activities
- failed to submit / complete two or more assignments correctly / on time or failed to review the material
- frequently had private conversations / disrupted / spoke during class activities
- willing to participate in discussions or activities when selected by teacher

__ **50) Struggling Student**
- repeatedly late to class / late from breaks / left early OR missed three classes
- often did not prepare / depended on classmates to complete assignments or rarely reviewed materials
- failed to submit / complete two or more assignments correctly / on time or failed to review the material
- frequently had private conversations / disrupted / spoke during class activities
- resisted interacting or withdrew, seemed unmotivated or uninterested in class activities

__ **0) Absent Student**
- inattentive, disruptive, unprepared OR missed four or more classes

Adams, J. W. 1988. You and Your Hearing Impaired Child. Washington, DC: Gallaudet Press.

Baker, Mona. 1993. In Other Words. New York, NY: Routledge.

Battison R. 1978. Lexical Borrowing in American Sign Language. Silver Spring, MD: Linstok Press.

Bloom, F. E. & A. Lazerson. 1988. Brain, Mind, and Behavior: Second Edition. New York, NY: W. H. Freeman and Company.

Bonvilliam, N. 1993. Language, Culture, and Communication: The Meaning of Messages (Second Edition). Upper Saddle River, NJ: Prentice Hall.

Bragg, B. & E. Bergman. 1989. Lessons in Laughter: The Autobiography of a Deaf Actor. Washington, DC: Gallaudet University Press.

Bragg, B. & E. Bergman. 1981. Tales From A Clubroom. Washington, DC. Gallaudet College Press.

Brill, R. 1984. International Congress on education of the Deaf: An Analytical History 1878 - 1980. Washington, DC: Gallaudet College Press.

Carruth, G. 1987. The Encyclopedia of American Facts & Dates. New York, NY: Harper and Row.

Cerney, B. 1996. "Language Acquisition, Language Teaching, and the Interpreter as a Model for Language Input" RID 1995 National Convention Proceedings. Silver Spring, MD: RID Publications.

Cerney, B. March, 2000. "Models and Paradigms" RID Views. Silver Spring, MD: RID Publications.

Cerney, B. March, 1996. "Don't Quit, We Need You" RID Views. Silver Spring, MD: RID Publications.

Cerney, B. February, 1996. "Interpreter Working Conditions: Sharing the Vision" RID Views. Silver Spring, MD: RID Publications.

Cerney, B. February, 1996. "Interpreters as Cultural Allies" RID Views. Silver Spring, MD: RID Publications.

Cerney, B. 1993. "The Self-Concept of Deaf Children in Residential and Mainstreamed Environments." Masters Thesis. University of Maryland.

Moores, D., Cerney, B., Garcia, M. 1991. School placement and least restrictive environment. In D. Moores, K. Meadow-Orlans (Eds.), Research in Education and Developmental Aspects of Deafness. Washington, DC: Gallaudet University Press.

Cerney, B. 1989. "The Deaf Adult Learner." Unpublished Manuscript. University of Maryland.

Cerney, B. 1987. "Numeral Incorporation in British Sign Language." Unpublished Manuscript. Gallaudet University.

Cerney, B. 1987. "A Reader's Guide to an International Study of Seven Signers." Unpublished Manuscript. Gallaudet University.

Christiansen, J. B. & S. N. Barnartt. 1995. Deaf President Now! The 1988 Revolution at Gallaudet University. Washington, DC: Gallaudet University Press.

Cokely, D., & C. Baker. 1980. American Sign Language: A Teacher's Resource Text on Grammar and Culture. Silver Spring, MD: TJ Publishers, Inc.

Cokely D. 1992. Interpretation: A Sociolinguistic Model. Burtonsville, MD: Linstok Press.

Cokely D. (Ed.) 1992. Sign Language Interpreters and Interpreting. Burtonsville, MD: Linstok Press.

Cornett, R. O. & M. E. Daisey. 1992. The Cued Speech Resource Book For Parents of Deaf Children. Raleigh, NC: National Cued Speech Association.

Costello, E. 1998. Random House Webster's American sign Language Dictionary. New York, NY: Random House.

Crabtree, M. & J. Powers, Eds. Language Files: Materials for an Introduction to Language. Columbus Ohio: Ohio State University Press.

Crosby, O. 1995. Silent Dancing: A Journey of Discovery. Park City, UT: Osmond Crosby.

Crystal, D. 1987. The Cambridge Encyclopedia of Language. New York, NY: Cambridge University Press.

Eastman, G. 1997 Sign Me Alice & Laurent Clerc: A Profile. Dawn Sign Press.

Fant, L. 1990. Silver Threads: A Personal Look at the First Twenty-five Years of the Registry of Interpreters for the Deaf. Silver Spring, MD: RID Press.

Fant, L. 1983. The American Sign Language Phrase Book. Chicago, IL: Contemporary Books, Inc.

Fleetwood, E., & M. Metzger. 1990. Cued Speech Transliteration: Theory and Application. Silver Spring, MD: Calliope Press.

Fleetwood, E. & M. Metzger. 1998. Cued Language Structure: An Analysis of Cued American English Based on Linguistic Principles.

Frishberg, N. 1990. Interpreting: An Introduction. Silver Spring, MD: RID Press.

Gallaudet, E. M. 1881. Resolutions of the Milan convention. American Annals of the Deaf, 26.

Gallaudet, E. M. 1983. History of the College for the Deaf: 1857 - 1907. Washington, DC: Gallaudet College Press.

Gannon, J. 1989. The Week the World Heard Gallaudet. Washington, DC: Gallaudet University Press.

Gannon, J. 1981. Deaf Heritage: A Narrative History of Deaf America. Silver Spring, MD: National Association of the Deaf.

Gebron J. 1996. Sign the Speech: An Introduction to Theatrical Interpreting. Hillsboro, OR: Butte Publications, Inc.

Groce, N. E. 1985. Everyone Here Spoke Sign Language: Hereditary Deafness on Martha's Vineyard. Cambridge, MA: Harvard University Press.

Haas, Christopher, Earl Fleetwood & Mike Ernest. 1995. An analysis of ASL variation within Deafblind interaction: Question forms, backchanneling, and turn-taking. In Communication Forum 1995. L. Byers, J. Chaiken, & M. Mueller, Eds. Washington, DC: Gallaudet University School of Communication.

Humphrey J. & B. Alcorn. 1994. So You Want to Be an Interpreter: An Introduction to Sign Language Interpreting. Salem, OR: Sign Enhancers, Inc.

Humphries, T., C. Padden, & T.J. O'Rourke. 1994. A Basic Course in American Sign Language, Second Edition. Silver Spring, MD: TJ Publishers, Inc.

Kaplan, H, S. Bally, & C. Garretson. 1985. Speechreading: A Way to Improve Understanding. Washington, DC: Gallaudet University Press.

Kageleiry, Jamie. 1999. The island that spoke by hand. Yankee. March: 48-55.

Kisor, H. 1990. What's That Pig Outdoors? A Memoir of Deafness. New York, NY: Penguin Books.

Klina, E. & U. Bellugi. 1979. The Signs of Language. Cambridge, MA: Harvard University Press.

Lane, H. 1984. When the Mind Hears: A History of the Deaf. New York: Random House.

Lane, H. 1992. The Mask of Benevolence: Disabling the Deaf Community. New York: Alfred A. Knopf.

Lane, H., R. Hoffmeister, & B. Bahan. 1996. A Journey into the DEAF-WORLD. San Diego, CA: Dawn Sign Press.

Lucas, Ceil, & Clayton Valli. 1992. Language Contact in the American Deaf Community. San Diego, CA: Academic Press.

Maher, J. 1993. William C. Stokoe, Jr. Deaf Life, January.

McIntire, M. 1986. Interpreting: The Art of Cross Cultural Mediation - Proceedings of the Ninth National Convention of the Registry of Interpreters for the Deaf July 4-8, 1985. Silver Spring, MD: RID Publications.

Neisser, A. 1983. The Other Side of Silence: Sign Language and the Deaf Community in America. Washington, DC: Gallaudet University Press.

Nettles, C. 1999. Proceedings of the Sixteenth National Convention of the Registry of Interpreters for the Deaf August 2-7, 1999. Silver Spring, MD: RID Publications.

O'Brien, Stephanie & Candace Steffen. 1996. Tactile ASL: ASL as used by Deafblind persons. In Communication Forum 1996. L. Byers & M. Rose, Eds. Washington, DC: Gallaudet University School of Communication.

Padden, C. and T. Humphries. 1988. Deaf in America: Voices from a Culture. Cambridge, MA: Harvard University Press.

RID. 1996. RID 1995 National Convention Proceedings. Silver Spring, MD: RID Publications.

RID. 1995. A Confluence of Diverse Relationships: Proceedings of the Thirteenth National Convention of the Registry of Interpreters for the Deaf August 10-14, 1993. Silver Spring, MD: RID Publications.

Sacks, O. 1989. Seeing Voices: A Journey into the World of the Deaf. Berkeley, CA: University of California Press.

Sauerburger, D. 1993. Independence Without Sight or Sound: Suggestions for Practitioners Working with Deaf-Blind Adults. New York, NY: American Foundation for the Blind.

Schuchman, J. S. 1989. Hollywood Speaks: Deafness and the film Entertainment Industry. Urbana, IL: University of Illinois Press.

Schwartz, Sue. 1996. Choices in Deafness: A Parent's Guide to Communication Options. Washington, DC: Gallaudet Press.

Seal, B. C. 1998. Best Practices in Educational Interpreting. Needham Heights, MA: Allyn & Bacon.

Seleskovitch D & M. Lederer. 1978. A Systematic Approach to Teaching Interpretation. Washington, DC: Pen and Booth.

Seleskovitch D. 1989. Interpreting for International Conferences: Problems of Language and Communication. Silver Spring, MD: RID Publications.

Snell, R. S. 1978. Atlas of Clinical Anatomy. Boston, MA: Little, Brown, and Company.

Smith, C., E. M. Lentz & K. Mikos. 1988. Signing Naturally: Level 1. San Diego, CA: Dawn Sign Press.

Smith, C., E. M. Lentz & K. Mikos. 1988. Signing Naturally: Level 2. San Diego, CA: Dawn Sign Press.

Smith, T. 1994. Guidelines: Practical Tips for Working and Socializing with Deaf-Blind People. Burtonsville, MD: Linstok Press.

Solow S.N. 1981. Sign Language Interpreting: A Basic Resource Book. Silver Spring, MD: National Association of the Deaf.Stokoe, W. 1960. Sign Language Structure: An Outline of the Visual Communication Systems of the American Deaf. Burtonsville, MD: Linstok Press.

Stokoe, W. 1965. The Dictionary of American Sign Language. Burtonsville, MD: Linstok Press.

Stokoe, W. 1969. Sign language diglossia.Studies in Linguistics 21: 27-41.

Supalla, S. 1991. Manually Coded English: The modality question in signed language development. In P. Siple & S. Fischer, (Eds.), Theoretical Issues in Sign Language Research. Chicago, IL: The University of Chicago Press.

Supalla, S. & B. Bahan. 1992. ASL Literature Series: Student Workbook & Videotext. Dawn Sign Press: San Diego, CA

Tennant, Richard & Marianne Gluszak Brown. 1998. The American Sign Language Handshape Dictionary. Washington,: Clerc Books (Gallaudet University Press).

VanCleve, J. V. & B. A. Crouch. 1989. A Place of Their Own: Creating the Deaf Community in America. Washington, DC: Gallaudet University Press.

Valli, C. & C. Lucas. 1995. Linguistics of American Sign Language: Revised Edition. Washington, DC: Gallaudet Press.

Winefield, R. 1987. Never the Twain Shall Meet: Bell, Gallaudet, and the Communications Debate. Washington, DC: Gallaudet University Press.

Wilcox, S., Ed. 1992. American Deaf Culture: An Anthology. Burtonsville, MD: Linstok Press.

Woodward, James C. 1972. Implications for sociolinguistic research among the deaf. Sign Language Studies 1: 1-7.

Woodward, James C. 1973. Some characteristics of Pidgin Sign English. Sign Language Studies 3: 39-46.